Spending
the kids'
inheritance

If you want to know how …

Holiday Courses for Long Weekends and Short Breaks
*A guide to the best holiday courses and workshops
in the UK and Ireland*

Buying a Property in France
*Honest independent advice you can't do without when buying a
property in France*

How to Make Your Own Will
*Covers the things a solicitor would tell you if you could afford to pay
for the time it would take*

Tracking Down Your Ancestors
*Discover the story behind your ancestors and bring your
family history to life*

Practical books that inspire

Send for a copy of the latest catalogue to:

How To Books
Spring Hill House, Spring Hill Road,
Oxford OX5 1RX, United Kingdom
info@howtobooks.co.uk
www.howtobooks.co.uk

Spending
the kids'
inheritance

How to ensure you have the
time of your life in retirement

2nd Edition

Annie Hulley

howtobooks

Published by How To Books Ltd
Spring Hill House, Spring Hill Road,
Oxford, OX5 1RX, United Kingdom
Tel: (01865) 375794. Fax: (01865) 379162
info@howtobooks.co.uk
www.howtobooks.co.uk

First edition 2006
Second edition 2008

British Library Cataloguing in Publication Data
A catalogue record for this book is available from the British
Library

ISBN 978 1 84528 291 2

Cover design by Baseline Arts Ltd, Oxford
Cartoons © Colin Shelbourn, www.shelbourn.com
Produced for How to Books by Deer Park Productions,
Tavistock, Devon
Typeset by Pantek Arts Ltd, Maidstone, Kent
Printed and bound by Cromwell Press Ltd, Trowbridge, Wiltshire

NOTE: The material contained in this book is set out in good
faith for general guidance and no liability can be accepted for
loss or expense incurred as a result of relying in particular
circumstances on statements made in this book. Laws and
regulations may be complex and liable to change, and readers
should check the current position with the relevant
authorities before making personal arrangements.

Contents

Acknowledgements

I would like to thank the following for their invaluable help in writing this book: Chris Clough, Sylvia Hulley, Maureen O'Connor, John Stillitz, Annette Donovan, Simon Whalley, Brenda Scott. Pam and David Bates, Silvia and Jacques. Joy and Ray Cox.

For Sylvia

Introduction

Everyone is living longer . . . well into their 80s . . . so you might have to 'Spend The Kids' Inheritance' (SKI) in order to survive. Our Edwardian ancestors did not enjoy the longevity that we do and it is becoming clear that a life of 'toil today with the hope of rest tomorrow' is no longer practicable. An ageing population puts a burden on society as a whole, particularly the young and it seems unlikely that the off-spring of the 'SKI' generation will be able to enjoy the same 'golden age' as their parents did.

However, those that have retired, are enjoying the freedom that being 'empty nesters' and mortgage free brings and this has given them a new zest for life. They feel they have the right to reward themselves for a lifetime of hard work, by enjoying new experiences such as travel, sport, cultural pursuits and indulging in big purchases, such as cars, second homes and exotic holidays.

Although there is a lot of focus on pensioner poverty, with one in three pensioners living on less than £150 per week, the fact is that two thirds of pensioners are not on the poverty line and some are very affluent indeed. Over 280,000 pensioners have assets of half a million or more. These pensioners are worth £240 billion, collectively! Pensioners hold nearly a tenth of all personal wealth in the UK. Most of this wealth is tied up in shares, bonds, unit trusts and is also invested in housing both within the UK and overseas. Many pensioners are active with their investments and have liquid assets worth in the region of £120 billion. They also have valuable possessions such as art, furniture and jewellery which can account for a further 10% of their wealth. They have amassed these small fortunes, not through being frugal but through the benefits of rising house prices, rising share prices, free university education and risk free pensions.

There is evidence to support the theory that today's retirees are spending their assets at a much faster rate than their predecessors did. In a recent report it was found that the over 50s market, is Europe's fastest-growing demographic. It reportedly holds more than 75% of the continent's wealth and accounts for approximately 50% of its consumer spending. Other findings show that men over the age of 60 are the key new consumers of cosmetics and that last year the average age of a first-time Harley-Davidson buyer was 59!

'Spending The Kids' Inheritance', which started out as a tongue-in-cheek slogan in the US, is fast becoming a reality both in America and the UK. Leaving an inheritance is a primary goal for only about 10% of the population and a growing number of financial advisers counsel older people against designing a 'retirement plan' for the express purpose of leaving an inheritance. These experts warn that longer life spans, steady inflation and growth in living standards, force most people to use their assets during their lifetime. This advice, coupled with the fact that SKI's believe that they have spent enough on their kids bringing them up (the latest figures estimate that it costs on average £166,000 to bring up a child in the UK) has made SKI's determined to squeeze as much out of the remainder of their lives as possible, regardless of the impact it has on 'the pot' at the end. Indeed the majority of beneficiaries from inheritance stand to gain only small sums, as large inheritances are limited to a few very lucky individuals, making inheritance distribution highly unequal.

Not all of us subscribe to the 'SKI' theory, but the reality is that many in retirement have not saved enough to support their lifestyles. In the UK alone there is a looming £57 billion annual 'black hole' in the amount being set aside for pension provision. It is clear that planning for retirement is a factor that needs to be 'shoe horned' into modern living practices as early as possible in order to avoid poverty in old age. With the pension crisis looming, it increases the need for a radical review of the working patterns of our lives. Not just by deferring the age of retirement to 67 or 69, but also by changing our working practices as a whole, by introducing flexible hours, career breaks and a 'work to live' policy rather than 'live to work' one.

We all want to be able to leave something in 'the pot' for our kids, let's be honest. Not many of us actually want to spend all the kid's inheritance but we do want to enjoy ourselves too. With careful planning and research the chances of poverty in retirement can be minimised and it is possible to have both your 'cake and eat it', by making sound investments in property, pensions, shares, Gilts, Fixed Income Investments, Commercial Property Funds and Corporate Bonds amongst other forms of investment.

So take your time and explore all the options . . . as what you decide to do later . . . could affect your planning now.

1

Young at Heart

You're not old until your 80 . . . that is the new theory and with that comes the belief that old age has been postponed . . . not indefinitely but certainly for longer than before. The age group now deemed as old (those in their 80s) and those that are deemed to be entering the first stage of aging (those in their 50s) leave an age span between them of 30 years. This long period of time will be an important decision making one. Things to consider could be:

♦ Where will you live, what will you do?
♦ When you retire will you retire completely?

- Will you sell up, stay put, downsize, move abroad, move nearer the kids?
- Choose a pied-à-terre or a rural retreat?
- What about pensions, allowances, finances?
- Will you want to travel? An interesting fact is that nearly as many 'oldies' are taking gap years as are students.
- Or take up a new hobby such as golf, sailing, art?
- And most importantly will you have the health and the money to be able to fulfil your dreams?

GOLDEN OLDIES

Don't worry you are not alone – everyone is getting older, even young people. But if you feel you are past it then consider Mick Jagger, Paul MaCartney, Twiggy, David Bowie, Cliff Richard, Elton John, Cilla Black, Barbara Streisand, Steven Spielberg, Raquel Welch, Alex Ferguson to name but a few . . . are all past it too. Life begins at 50 and you'd better believe it!

SILVER SURFERS

It is vital to get on the 'net', as without it you really will be at a disadvantage when it comes to sourcing holidays, courses and virtually everything. I have tried my best when writing this book to include telephone numbers as well as websites but it has not always been possible. It is reported that 'Silver Surfers' in the UK currently spend an average of ten hours a week on the Internet. 70% of them use the Internet to research holidays and make travel arrangements. They are also more likely to use the Internet for shopping than the younger generations. Some of them have even created their own websites and 17% are part of an online community. Other uses that the over 50s 'surf the net' for are to research medical conditions and 'on-line' learning opportunities. Many 'silver surfers' who live alone find the net a companion as they log onto key sites for the over 50s and chat on-line and e-mail each other. So my advice here is if you don't aim to achieve anything else in retirement then at least 'get on-line'.

'GREYS' AND GADGETS

Far from being afraid of modern technology the over 50s positively embrace it. In a recent survey over half of the over 50s said that they own at least one of the following products: desktop PC, Internet access, satellite TV, DVD player, cordless phone, mobile phone and a digital camera. They also spend the most time (over 20 hours) a week watching television. Innovative technology is a part of their everyday lives and 72% of the over 50s surveyed said they would not be happy if all the digital and computer technology was no longer available.

RETIREMENT DEVELOPMENTS

As the population ages, retirement opportunities are expanding. The 'grey pound' has tempted housing developers into finding new exciting ways of catering to the ever growing demands of those entering their 'third act'. Retirement villages and retirement apartments are now becoming the way of the future. They offer independence, security and 24-hour help, along with many other facilities for the more mature 'consumer' to enjoy. These developments embrace the concept that whilst those in their 50s and above may not be at their physical peak, there is no need for them to compromise on their lifestyle. They can still enjoy all the benefits of independent living without the onerous responsibilities of house maintenance, health and security issues.

NOT JUST FOR THE WEALTHY

In fact the opportunities for retirement living are greater now than they have ever been and these opportunities are not limited to the wealthy alone. There are many schemes which now offer mortgage opportunities to those who would previously have been excluded, because of age.

STAYING PUT

You may choose to stay in your own home and have no immediate plans to do anything other than carry on as before, until you may have to make a choice. There are certainly many ways of adapting the home to changing needs and there are several grants available from your local social services to facilitate this, as it is always cheaper and most effective to keep people in their own homes rather than having to re-house them in a care home. There is of course the popular 'halfway housing' that is known as sheltered accommodation and this type of accommodation has many advantages both for enjoying an active retirement (peace of mind when you are away) but also for a less active retirement, with help being on hand should you need it.

TRAVELLING OVERSEAS

Your dream may be to travel extensively or you may want to retire abroad. There are many ways of achieving both these ambitions but it is important that you do extensive research to make sure that you are fully prepared for what travel may offer you or whether to settle overseas and abandon the British way of life is actually for you. As with any important decision, retirement choices have to be fully researched and the more you know the better off you will be.

LIVING THE DREAM AND KEEPING FIT

Whether it is your wish to retire overseas, have a cottage in the country, a place by the sea or a pied-à-terre in town, this book intends to explore ways to achieve these dreams and make them into reality. It also plans to look at ways of keeping 'young at heart' and other things to consider for a healthy and happy retirement such as:

- Exercise/aerobics/cardiovascular and for just keeping in trim.
- Learning something new to keep you on your toes.
- Eating healthily.

- Having a social life and making the effort to go out and do things.
- Having fun, thinking young and growing old fulfilled.

SEMI-RETIRED/CAREER CHANGES

Maybe your dream retirement is to keep on working until you drop and the thought of being at home all day sends you into a decline. There is no law that says you have to stop working, obviously some occupations stipulate a retirement age, but there may still be job opportunities out there that can make use of your existing skills on a consultancy basis. Or maybe you are still in your 50s and fancy a career change such as running a pub or a B&B either in the UK or overseas. Or alternatively you may want to change your life completely and do something worthwhile to help others, be it working in a charity shop or doing voluntary work overseas. Whatever it is you want to do, as long as you have got health on your side and the necessary finances to follow your choices, then there is no reason why the latter stage of your life shouldn't be the most rewarding.

FULL TIME RETIREMENT

So you've retired . . . that moment you have been looking forward to all your working life has finally arrived. It's your final day at work and then that's it: a lifetime of freedom . . . a pension, free bus pass, help with your heating, help with your council tax and nothing to do all day except watch Richard and Judy – perfect!

If that's how you think then this will not be the book for you. If, however, you feel that you are not ready for the scrap heap just yet and are ready for a challenge, then read on. Retirement is not about giving up, its more about moving onto the next stage of your life. It's the icing on the cake after a lifetime of hard work . . . so it's important to make the most of those retirement years!

2

Where to Live

Choosing where to retire is an important 'life decision'. The right retirement choice can lead to years of contentment but the wrong choice can be distressing and costly, so it is important that you consider carefully what type of property you want, where you want to be located and whether you might want to move again.

An alternative to going it alone is 'Retirement Housing' which is now the preferred term used to describe Leasehold Sheltered Housing, also known as Private Sheltered Housing. The aim of retirement housing is to allow the occupants to live life to the full, without the hassle of house maintenance issues but with the benefits of additional support and security if and when required.

THE ELDERLY ACCOMMODATION COUNCIL (EAC)

The database from the EAC estimated that there are 103,000 units already built and over 80% of these are privately developed. The major developers for this sector of housing are McCarthy & Stone, Pegasus, Bovis, Churchill and English Courtyard.

Examples

The retirement schemes researched in this book are offered up as examples only and range from apartments . . . to living in a country mansion . . . to living in a retirement village . . . to living in a Continuing Care Retirement Scheme. There are so many schemes available, that only personal research will help you decide what you want. Some things to consider before making your choice are outlined below.

Location

Where the development is situated is vital when making your choice of retirement home. A lot of people choose to move nearer to their families and it is worth bearing in mind that if you choose to retire elsewhere it may prove difficult for your family to visit. The key here is how accessible do you want to be to your nearest and dearest. When choosing where to live, it is worth bearing in mind some of the following:

- city/town profile
- arts and cultural activities
- recreation and outdoor activities
- continuing education opportunities
- services for the elderly
- hospitals/doctors/medical facilities

- airports
- local shops
- distance to nearby cities
- public transport links.

Shops

How close you are to amenities will also be an important consideration, particularly if you no longer have use of a car. A good test will always be how far you have to walk to get a pint of milk and a newspaper. Other useful shops to have within walking distance would be a supermarket, chemist, post office and hairdressers.

Doctors

Retirement developments, as a whole, will most likely not have a doctor on call, although retirement villages may sometimes have their own surgery. You will need to consider when you register with a practice whether or not you will be able to walk to it, drive, or need to use public transport or any Dial-A-Ride scheme. It will also be worth checking with surgeries in the immediate area of a retirement home whether they are taking on new patients, as you can sometimes find that their books are closed!

Public transport

As with any purchase of a property, its proximity to good public transport links is vital (unless you are opting for that isolated rural retreat). You may find that you depend on public transport more and more, especially given the fact that a lot of public transport is free for pensioners.

City living

Many retirees are choosing to move back into city centres. This can be for all sorts of reasons such as being close to restaurants, theatres and shopping centres. Other attractions are museums, art galleries and places of architectural and historical interest. The advantages of city living are many and if you want to 'Spend The Kids' Inheritance' then being in the hub of a city centre and enjoying all it has to offer is a good place to be. The downside to city living is the noise, the litter and the crime but if you find yourself a secure retirement apartment these should be less of a problem.

What is a retirement apartment?

A retirement apartment is a place where you can live independently, whilst having help on hand should you need it. Even if you don't, it's reassuring to know help is there. The whole concept of retirement developments is that they take the stress out of living alone. The same applies to couples who are reaching an age where anything to do with DIY or house maintenance is reaching be a bit of a headache. In essence, it affords you total 'living' independence, whilst being maintenance free.

What extra benefits can I expect from a retirement development?

These will depend on what development you choose. In general you can expect there to be some, if not all of the following:

- house manager
- emergency call, door entry and fire alarm systems
- maintained communal gardens
- communal car park
- communal lounge
- laundry room
- guest room (for visitors)
- lift
- hairdressing salon
- restaurant

- swimming pool
- keep fit facilities.

What kind of things should I be looking for when making my choice of retirement home?

Safety and security are important aspects as most people, particularly the elderly, want to feel secure in their environment. Most retirement developments should be able to provide this via door entry systems and intruder alarms. Some schemes allow you to be able to see your visitors through CCTV on a designated channel on your TV set. This enables you to monitor who you are allowing into the building. As well as the statutory smoke alarms, the building will be fitted with a comprehensive fire alarm system, generally directly linked to the fire station. This, of course, will be regularly maintained and tested.

Monitoring system

Retirement apartments will generally have a monitoring system, activated by pull cords or buttons which are easily accessible in each room in case of an emergency. This monitoring system will enable you to get help, should you need it, either from the house manager, or if he/she is not on duty, some other monitoring service such as 'Careline'. This will allow you to have peace of mind knowing that help is on hand. It will also be a great source of comfort to your family to know that you will not be left helpless should an emergency occur.

The house manager

The house manager plays a very important part, not only in the day-to-day running of the development, but also in planning social activities as well as being your first port of call if there is a problem. House managers will obviously differ in the way they carry out their duties. Some may be particularly good at the maintenance issues, whilst others may put more emphasis on the social side of things. You should consider meeting the house manager before purchasing your apartment to ask them about what role they play in the development and what their hours of duty are (as they will have a life too!). It is important if you are hoping to generate a social life for yourself that you are aware what organised events the house manager encourages and supports. Most people moving into retirement schemes are generally leaving their old life behind and for some this can be an unsettling time. A sympathetic and friendly house manager can make all the difference during this transitional period. They will also play a vital role in helping you integrate with the other residents and get to know people when you first move in.

Facilities

The communal facilities are something else to consider. Are the gardens pleasant and well maintained? Is the communal lounge comfortable and spacious? Is there a laundry room and is it well equipped? Are there parking facilities for your visitors? Is there a guest room and does it have en-suite facilities? Is there a communal kitchen area to make tea and coffee if you feel like a chat? All these are important considerations when choosing a retirement home. However, it is also important to remember that the more facilities a development has, the more expensive the service charge will be.

Take your time

Try to spend some time in the communal lounge. Ask the sales assistant to make you a cup of tea and allow yourself time to sit down and muse as to whether you find the ambience pleasing. The most important thing is, as with any property, is not to be rushed into a purchase. Take your time and ask to see as many apartments as possible that suit your requirements. Don't worry about inconveniencing the sales assistants as they are there to help you find the right apartment and you want to make sure that you have made the right choice. It would be disappointing to discover after moving in that you wish you had chosen another apartment.

Aspect/position

You may well spend some time as an elderly person looking out of your window so it is important to consider the aspect of the property. For instance, if it is situated on the ground floor behind the car park, would you be happy staring at cars coming and going all day? If it is on the street side, would you be content with the possibility of people peering in and could you cope with traffic noise? If you are considering an apartment on the ground floor, what are the security aspects? Do you mind sleeping at night with your windows closed and if there are window locks are they secure enough to give you peace of mind? If you are choosing an apartment on the higher floor, you will have to consider whether you are happy getting into the lift. You will need to check that the lift is fitted with the correct alarms in case of an emergency. Also, consider how far away the apartment is from the lift and imagine what it would be like to walk from the lift to the apartment with a bag of shopping, for example, or how easy it is to push your shopping trolley down the corridor.

Pets

You may have a cat or a dog that you want to bring with you so it is most important to check with the management company, via the sales assistant, whether they will allow you to do this. If it is allowed, what restrictions will there be?

Management company

A management company, on behalf of the freeholder, will manage the development. They will be responsible for the day-to-day running of the development, including hiring the services of the house manager. It will be their collective responsibility to ensure that the development is properly maintained and all management issues run smoothly. You will need to pay the annual service charge to this company and it is worth your while investigating fully what those service charges entail. It will also be important to find out whether the managing agents keep separate bank accounts for the development, so that all costs are clearly monitored. It is also worth asking whether you will be permitted to check the accounts. Does the company hold annual accounts and budget meetings to discuss service charges for the year ahead? The management company should be able to account for all service charge expenditure and produce receipts for inspection by residents. Ask to see copies of the service charges for the last few years, to see if there have been any significant increases. Obviously how far back these accounts go will depend on the age of the development. If you are unsure about any of the accounts ask your legal adviser to check these out for you.

The Association of Retirement Housing Managers (ARHM)

The management company should be a member of the ARHM, which is the trade body for the industry and it should operate within their codes of practice. Members of the association should be able to provide you with a comprehensive Purchaser Information Pack (PIP) to assist your property purchase.

What is the purpose of the ARHM?

The organisation sets standards for management companies who manage (mainly leasehold) privately owned retirement dwellings. ARHM's Policy Officer, John Mills, says

The secret of ARHM's success has been a recognition across the whole retirement housing sector that poor management standards, which were common in retirement housing ten or fifteen years ago, were threatening to damage the public perception of the whole sector. This shared interest has driven management companies to pool their experience and join forces. The aim being to drive up management standards for the benefit of all and most of all, for the benefit of retired leaseholders themselves.

For more information on the role of the ARHM tel: 020 7463 0660, visit www.arhm.org or e-mail enquiries @arhm.org

◆ For specialist independent advice on services available to leasehold-ers contact AIMS (Advice, Information and Mediation Service). This is part of Age Concern. Tel: 020 8765 7465 or e-mail aims@ace.org.uk
◆ For legal rights for leaseholders contact LEASE. Tel: 0845 345 1933 or visit their website www.lease-advice.org
◆ A leaflet on extra care retirement housing is available from Housing LIN. Tel: 020 7820 1682.

Contingency fund

This fund is usually a part of the service charge that is put aside into a separate account to help cover any redecoration costs and major repair work that needs to be undertaken. Or, if any of the equipment needs to be replaced, such as washing machines if there is a laundry room. It is worth checking whether the contingency fund is adequate to meet any future expenditure and if not, what is the short fall likely to be? Obviously the managing agents cannot plan for the unexpected, but it is only prudent for them to have some reserves in case of any costly emer-gencies that are not covered by the building insurance.

Financial considerations

There will be considerable savings on heating and electricity bills, as your retirement home will most likely be smaller and more energy effi-cient than your existing home. It will also be important for you to understand what is not covered by the service charge which will proba-bly be the internal maintenance and decoration of your own apartment as well as your contents insurance. You will also have to pay all the util-ity bills and council tax for your own apartment.

Accommodation

There will be a lot of things to take into consideration when choosing what type of accommodation you require and most retirement developments will have been designed to suit the needs of the elderly. In particular, how accessible the development is will be a key factor. Will it be easy to get around? Are the kitchens well equipped and do the bathrooms have walk in showers or baths with hand rails, making them easy to get in and out of? If the bathrooms do not have a shower, would it be easy to install one at a later date, should the need arise? Are the taps easy to turn and do they have easy grip handles? Another thing to check is the position of the electrical sockets, as in most retirement homes they are situated off the ground level, making it unnecessary to bend down to plug things in. Check the emergency call facilities in each room. Are they easy to reach and is there a call button situated in the bathroom? Most importantly, do you like the apartment and its position within the development? Most of the doorways will be slightly wider than you are used to, in order to accommodate wheelchair, should it be necessary.

Furniture

You will also notice that most apartments will be smaller than you are used to. If you are moving from a large house you will obviously need to sell or give away some of your furniture. This can be a bit of an emotional roller coaster, as indeed the move itself will be, but you do not want to move into your new apartment only to find that you have too much furniture and not enough room to move around. It might be worth considering sending some of your furniture to auction and using any money gained from the sale towards purchasing some new furniture, which would be of a more practical size in a smaller apartment. If you are in any doubt about what will fit and what won't, study the floor plans carefully and take measurements of your furniture. Another problem could be that on removal day, you may find that the large sofa you have always had will not actually be able to fit into the apartment . . . so it is well worth getting that tape measure out!

The show flat

You will be able to look around a show flat if the development is new. Be aware that the show flat will probably have furniture that is much smaller than yours. It may be worth investigating if the furniture is available for sale through a specialist company. Ask the sales assistant for advice about this, should you want to choose this option.

Case study: Mulberry Court, Bedford Road, East Finchley, London N2 9DZ

Mulberry Court is a development of retirement apartments built by McCarthy & Stone, who are the largest and longest established providers of retirement homes. The development is close to all amenities and has the added advantage of good transport links and easily accessible shops.

Development specification

- Residents' lounge
- Security entry system
- Guest suite
- Car park on site
- Garden
- Resident house manager
- Emergency call system
- Lift to all floors
- Fire detection equipment
- Laundry room
- Roof terrace

Apartment specification

- Fitted kitchen with integrated fridge-freezer and ceramic hob
- Under pelmet lighting

- Fitted and fully tiled bathroom with shower over bath
- 24 hour Careline points in each main room
- Camera entry system for use with standard TV
- Double glazing
- Electric slimline heaters
- Intruder alarm
- Easy grip lever taps
- Heated towel rail
- Fitted wardrobe in master bedroom
- Telephone point in living room and main bedroom
- Balconies to selected apartments

Management

One company dominates the management of retirement housing and that is Peverel Management Services, part of the Peverel Group. It provides services to almost half of the retirement housing sector. Other providers are Guardian Management services, part of Anchor Trust, followed by the Retirement Care Corporation and Hanover Property Management.

Extra Care Estates

Extra Care Estates have been built for homeowners for the last fifteen years and are sold using terms such as 'very sheltered', 'assisted living', 'close care' or 'fully serviced'. The main providers are Bovis, McCarthy & Stone and Retirement Security. There are approximately 127 schemes calling themselves 'Extra Care' and they are either sold outright or are part of a shared ownership scheme.

I have chosen my apartment, what is the next step?

- In order to reserve the apartment of your choice, you will be asked to hand over a non-returnable reservation fee. This is generally in the region of £1,000 to £2,000.
- If you are selling your own home, you will need to appoint an estate agent to assist with the sale.

▶

- You will need to appoint a solicitor to carry out the conveyance. Your solicitor can represent you for both your sale and purchase. Always ask for an estimate of what the solicitor's charges will be. If they are not prepared to give you an estimate of their charges then look for another solicitor!
- You may need the services of a financial adviser if you are considering taking out a mortgage. Please refer to Chapter 7 on Finance for further details.

Sales manager for Mulberry Court, John Stillitz, says:

I joined McCarthy & Stone after escaping from the frustrations of financial services - and what a revelation it was. Suddenly I was involved with a product in which I believed, talking to prospective buyers who wanted to be contacted and best of all, surrounded by the most charming and interesting people. As the development fills up, for me personally, the residents are by far my best marketing gizmo. It is often difficult for someone new coming into a retirement development for the first time to appreciate its true worth. Yes, they can see the apartment, the communal lounge and the garden and roof terrace. I will show them the laundry room and the guest room and explain the security and the care alarm systems and introduce them to the house manager, but it is only when people looking around meet the residents that the fun really starts. After the briefest introductions, friendships are quickly cemented, as experiences are shared. When a perspective buyer listens to a resident, it is so much more believable than a salesperson.

Case study: Maureen O'Connor, resident at Mulberry Court

It was a daunting prospect when I first knew that I would have to move to a small flat in busy London, away from my four bedroom home in Essex where I had raised my five children. My husband had suffered a severe stroke and needed permanent nursing home care and I was left alone at 78 in a large house difficult to maintain. Four of our children had moved to North London, so the obvious solution was to find a nursing home convenient for them all to visit, and for me to buy a small flat nearby. The move was quite traumatic, especially having to part with so many treasured possessions and I began to think life was almost at an end. Never for one moment did I envisage the extent to which the move would offer me a whole new lease of life. It was not long before I was comfortably settled in a new block of sheltered accommodation in East Finchley, which is within easy reach of all my family, who are now able to worry about me less because the development provides such good security, Careline facilities and a friendly house manager. The main advantage of this type of dwelling is that I can be completely independent, yet have back-up if necessary. My one bedroom flat is easily maintained and I am fortunate that the development's location means local shops are easily accessible. But most important of all, is the wonderful camaraderie which exists among the occupants. From the moment a person enters the main door of the building a feeling of warmth and comfort is generated throughout, and the welcoming residents' lounge is fast becoming a central point of activity. Coffee mornings, poetry and literary readings, games evenings, suppers, and even exercise classes, all add to the spirit of friendliness.

For all enquiries about Mulberry Court tel: 0208 815 9167. Current contact numbers for other McCarthy & Stone Developments are:

- South East office 0500 870454
- South West office 0800 919132

- Midlands office 0800 521276
- North West office 0500 006565
- Western office 0800 085 4798
- North London office 0800 027 2445
- Scottish office 0800 525271

UPSTAIRS/DOWNSTAIRS . . . LIVING IN A COUNTRY MANSION

Have you ever fancied 'Spending The Kids' Inheritance' living the dream? Servants below stairs, you 'lording' it above with a horse drawn carriage parked out the front, opposite the stable block! Well, back to reality. For most of us that is a dream that may never be realised, bar winning the lottery of course. However, if you are set on living in a 'country pile' then you may wish to consider a retirement development converted from a mansion or a grand old country house. Simon and Nigel Whalley run Historic House Retirement Homes Ltd (HHRH).

Historic House Retirement Homes Ltd

Simon Whalley explains the history of HHRH:

> The business was founded as a nursing home by my grandparents in the 1920s. Following on from our parents, my brother Nigel and I took over the management a few years ago and extended the range of services into 'Assisted Living' and then last year into 'Retirement Apartments', when we took over the 'Albury Park Mansion' from the Country Houses Association (CHA). The close involvement of a family team is fundamental to the 'country house' atmosphere we try to create in all our locations.

What services does HHRH provide?

- **Nursing care:** the provision of full care with nursing under registration for elderly patients at Birtley House Nursing Home.

◆ **Assisted living:** the provision of apartments owned individually under a lease, together with close assistance on a 24 hours a day basis. This is designed for independent living but with constant support and monitoring for elderly residents. This is provided at 'Birtley Mews' which is a new build development close to the Nursing Home.

◆ **Retirement apartments with support:** for retired but active and independent persons looking to buy into a secure environment that will provide support, if or when, they need it in the future. The target customer is someone with an independent lifestyle, comfortable personal circumstances and an appreciation of the 'historic country house' ambience. These apartments are situated in Albury Park.

Albury Park

Albury Park boasts Mews Cottages in its repertoire. The mews had been converted from a former stable block in the 1960s, but has recently been refurbished. They all have their own front doors which open out onto a south facing courtyard garden and have full access to the mansion's glorious six acres of grounds, which slope down to the River Tillingbourne.

History of Albury Park

The history of Albury Park is extensive and it was entered in the Domesday Book in 1086. From 1969 to 2004 the CHA owned the house until the Whalley's purchased it in 2004. Prior to this, the house had been in the ownership of the Percy family whose main estate lies in Alnwick, Northumberland. Until her death in 1965, the Dowager Duchess Helen, widow of Alan 8th Duke of Northumberland and mother of the 9th Duke, lived for a part of each year in the mansion at Albury.

Albury Park today

Today, in the ownership of the Whalley family the entrance hall, library and the drawing room remain as they have been for a hundred years or more, but the remainder of the house had already been converted by the CHA into 40 private apartments. The conversion work took over two years to complete and when Albury Park was re-opened in 1971 it became the home of some 50 residents. The Whalley's are currently refurbishing many of these apartments and, if you like the idea of living in a country mansion, this could be the place for you. Some of the apartments boast high ceilings and original features whilst others have spectacular views over the grounds. The outside appearance of the house is the design of the architect Pugin.

The apartments

You will need to be 55 or over to live in the apartments. They are not cheap and you will not technically own them as you will be required to pay a deposit for what is known as a 'lifetime license'. The license provides both security and flexibility. It is not for a fixed term and can be terminated, giving six months notice. The deposit is returnable at the end of this period. If mobility or health issues arise, the license is transferable to a more suitable location or the group nursing home. When transferring to the nursing home the deposit is repaid. For short-term illness the nursing home is available and the service charges at Albury are waived for the duration of the nursing home stay. Simon Whalley says 'the independence of residents is fully respected and every effort will be made to support them in the location of their choice, for as long as possible'.

Can there be any flexibility in the cost?

Costs can be tailored to specific circumstances. Although the deposit should not be regarded as a financial investment, it is possible to provide some opportunities for residents to gain a share in any increase in value after a period of years.

Service charges

These can vary but are currently from £1,500 to £3,000 for single occupancy per month. Second residents are normally charged 20% of the
monthly fee.

What is provided in the service charge?

◆ **Laundry:** a weekly laundry service for sheets and towels is included.
   In addition there are laundry facilities for residents to freely use on
   the premises.
◆ **Cleaning:** twice weekly cleaning and monthly window cleaning.
◆ **Maintenance:** use of grounds and public rooms.
◆ **Lunches:** are provided daily (additional meals at a small extra
   charge).
◆ **Minibus:** a minibus is provided for shopping trips and outings.
◆ **Heat/light/water/waste disposal:** are all included in the service
   charge.
◆ **Council tax:** this is not currently charged to individual residents but
   is subject to review.

Cottage residents can opt for a reduced service package, which does not
include meals, cleaning or laundry. All other services are included.

What can I expect HHRH to provide in the accommodation?

The apartments and cottages vary greatly in size and facilities can often
be tailored to individual requirements. There are one or two bedroom
properties available and some of them have two bathrooms/showers.
The apartments are unfurnished but will be carpeted, centrally heated
and provide adequate electric points and lighting. All have some form
of cooking facilities, whilst others have a fully equipped small kitchen.

What social activities are encouraged?

The brochure states that frequent concerts and events are hosted in the public rooms. Visits to the theatre and cinema are also organised, as are visits to specific events. Twice monthly there is a Sunday drinks 'get together'.

Who maintains the grounds and apartments?

The group's specialist team, 'Birtley Brook Estates', maintains the grounds. All cleaning and other maintenance issues are looked after by an 'in-house' team.

Are guestrooms provided for residents' visitors?

Guest suites are provided principally for the use of residents' guests but may sometimes be occupied on a short-term basis by outside persons. Some of the cottages may also be occupied by people younger than 55, on a 'reduced service' basis.

The 24-hour call system

There will always be a duty manager on call and a new call system has been installed to provide emergency response. General assistance can also be provided should you need to move any furniture.

Case study: Mrs Brenda Scott

Mrs Brenda Scott, aged 88, lives in the Coach House at Albury. She has lived there for seven years and was there when CHA owned Albury Mansion. She has remained in her home since the Whalley's purchased Albury in 2004.

My husband, a retired engineer, decided to build a house on the Island of Elba, where we lived for thirty-one years. When my husband reached the age of 90, we decided it was time to think about moving back to the UK. We had been members of the CHA for

some time and when we came back to the UK we stayed in the
Coach House at Albury originally on a temporary basis. However, my
husband decided that the Coach House would be a perfect solution
to our relocating back to the UK and we made enquiries with the
CHA about purchasing it on a 'lifetime lease' basis. This meant that
we put a capital sum down and then paid a monthly service charge.
The CHA were very patient with us, as it took eighteen months
before we eventually moved in. It is always difficult to decide what
to do when you have lived out of the UK for so long. Our children
were scattered and it was a great relief to me to be finally settled.
My husband sadly died three years ago but I have remained at
Albury. It suits me very well, as I feel very secure here and I enjoy
the company of others, although there are currently several of the
apartments unoccupied due to the management changeover. It is nice
to have a coffee after dinner in the drawing room and to mingle with
the other residents of Albury.

My visit to Albury

I visited Albury on a beautiful late summer's day and it is indeed
impressive. Simon Whalley kindly showed me around and I visited
some of the apartments. I was very impressed by what I saw and the
grounds are fantastic; abundant with ancient trees, a trickling stream
and rabbits and hares cavorting openly in the grounds (and eating the
flowers if they get the chance!). Obviously, living in a country mansion
does not come cheap and this arrangement may not suit most pockets as
it is, in essence, for the 'well heeled'. Living in the country might for
some be a dream, but for others it could prove to be too isolated, particularly if you do not drive, although there is the use of a mini bus for
trips into Guildford and other outings. The flats are conversions and not
purpose built, so you would have to accept that some of the rooms and
their layout might not necessarily have the advantages of a purpose built
retirement apartment. On the plus side, you are living in a unique

environment, steeped in history in a marvellous setting. There is also the advantage of a transfer to the nursing home at Birtley, should the need arise for permanent or respite care.

RURAL RETREATS

If you choose to live in the wilds of the countryside during your retirement 'far away from the madding crowd' and without the support of a retirement scheme, you will need to consider fully what being isolated may later come to mean. If you are in good health and enjoy driving then a rural retreat could be ideal for you. There are many advantages to living in the country, not least being that you can enjoy the beautiful countryside away from the stresses and strains of modern urban living. It is, however, important to consider that you may need to move again should mobility or health problems arise.

LIFETIME HOMES AND RETIREMENT VILLAGES

In 1991 the Lifetime Homes concept was developed by a group of housing experts who came together as the 'Joseph Rowntree Foundation Lifetime Homes Group'. Lifetime Homes have 16 design features that ensure a new flat or house will meet the demands of most households. This does not mean that the new home will be littered with gadgets that you have no need for. It means that the design of the home is flexible to meet the changes that you would have to make, if in later life you have mobility problems. Research suggests that not only will occupiers of the homes benefit but the taxpayer will also benefit to the tune of £5.5 billion over a 60-year period. These savings come from reduced expenditure on having to adapt a home and a reduction in need to move people into residential care.

What is the Joseph Rowntree Housing Trust?

The Joseph Rowntree Housing Trust, separately established in 1968, is a charity and a registered social landlord.

What is the target market for Lifetime Homes?

Lifetime Homes will be suitable for older people and for the vast majority of disabled people, as well as the non-disabled person. They will have a wider market of potential buyers, and because they are new build will have the edge on older properties when it comes to marketing.

Annette Donovan from Archstone Lifestyle Homes Ltd says:

The over 55 market is increasing with people wanting to buy a property that enables them to enjoy an active lifestyle, whilst avoiding the stress of maintenance and the worry of leaving a property if they go away for extended periods. It provides peace of mind and the enjoyment of living with like-minded neighbours.

Do the features designed for retirement living make homes more marketable?

The design features for retirement living do make the homes more marketable but in a subtle way. When walking into one of our Leisure Years Homes it is not obvious that the design features to aid future living are there. For example, there is space for turning a wheelchair in dining areas and living rooms and adequate provision for wheelchair users elsewhere. The living rooms are at entrance level and inhouses of two or more storeys there is space on the entrance level and that could be utilised as a convenient bed space. There are other design considerations and features in place so that residents can adapt their home to tailor it to their needs, should they later require it.

Do you achieve the specifications set out by the Rowntree Trust?

At the moment our designs don't provide for a reasonable route for a potential hoist from the main bedroom to the bathroom. The need for this may be limited however and we are currently looking into it. We do have a walk-in shower on the ground floor of the cottages, which is wheelchair accessible. It also has a WC and a wash basin and the dining room can easily be converted into a downstairs bedroom if necessary. Walls in bathrooms and toilets can withstand the addition of hand rails. Windows are at a lower height wherever possible, subject to local planning permission.

Can these features put people off of buying?

Yes and accordingly we have put in features discreetly, to avoid people feeling that they are being categorised.

Case study: Archstone Lifestyle Homes, Hayling Island

Hayling Island is where windsurfing was invented in 1958. There are still a lot of water sports available including: windsurfing, sailing and canoeing. Hayling Island covers ten square miles and is situated between Chichester and Langstone Harbour and has been inhabited since Roman times. Amenities include a theatre, leisure centre, golf course (par 3 links), marina, plenty of shops and restaurants. There is a strong sense of community in the area. It has award-winning beaches and remains relatively unspoilt by over development. Hayling Island is ten miles from Chichester where the Theatre Festival is held. Other shopping areas can easily be visited such as at Gunwharf Quays in Portsmouth. There is a ferry service between Hayling Island and Portsmouth. Twenty miles away is 'Goodwood Racecourse', which as well as horseracing, hosts other events all year round. In the last century the biggest export from Hayling Island was salt and it was estimated that 150 tons of salt would have been produced each season!

Fountain Square

Fountain Square is one of Archstone's developments and it comprises of 14 two or three bedroom cottages. The cottages are situated around a central courtyard and, as the name suggests, there is a fountain in the middle of it. The courtyard has been landscaped to provide seating areas and pergolas amongst an array of shrubs and flowers. Most of the cottages have a rear garden and some have a conservatory.

Where is it situated on Hayling Island?

Fountain Square is situated centrally on Haying Island and is within the area known as West Town, which provides a variety of shops and restaurants close by. In addition, the main shopping area 'Mengham' is a ten minute walk away.

Security/car parking

There are security gates and an estate manager who is there to keep an eye on things should you go away for any length of time. The electronic entrance gates link to the individual entry phone system. Also, within the gates are secure car parking ports for residents and visitors. There is also a communal car washing bay with outside tap and power point. The facility also has the usual specification of intruder and smoke alarms.

The specification for a typical cottage would include:

Kitchen:

- Quality kitchen units, worktops and tiling
- Electric oven, hob (choice of electric or gas) and extractor hood
- Integrated washer/dryer
- Cushioned floor and pelmet lighting
- Dishwasher

Lounge:

- TV/FM/satellite or cable point
- Telephone point
- Decorative fire surround and electric fire

Bathroom:

- White sanitary ware by Ideal Standard from the 'Alto' range
- Vanity unit/co-ordinated wall tiling
- Bath with thermostatic shower, lever taps and heated towel rail
- Mirror, light and shaver point

Bedroom:

- Built-in wardrobes with shelves and rail
- TV/FM/satellite point and telephone point

▶

Property management/estate manager/service charge

Broadleaf Management Services Ltd is a member of the ARHM and as such is bound by their code of conduct. They are responsible for all the maintenance issues regarding the communal areas and gardens. They are also responsible for external decoration (including personal cottages) and house insurance. It is their responsibility to hire the services of an estate manager. This is paid for out of the service charge and you are entitled to ask to see recent accounts to check up on what the expenditure on 'services' is likely to be.

Options and services

You may like the estate manager to look after your property if you are going away, or hire the services of a gardener. This can be arranged for a fee chargeable to you.

Emergency contact

Broadleaf can arrange for a telephone 'life-line' to be connected using your own personal telephone, or in the form of a brooch or pendant. This service is an optional extra and the cost of it would be charged to you.

Independence

Many of the cottages are designed to accommodate a stair lift should the need arise and this can be arranged through the estate manager or your custom liason officer. The custom liason officer is your contact, should there be anything wrong with your property for the first two years of occupancy, which forms part of the NHBC guarantee.

Where are the developments situated?

Archstone Lifestyle Homes Developments in the southern counties include Ilminster in Somerset, Alresford and Fleet in Hampshire, Verwood in Dorset, Branksome Park and Lower Parkstone in Poole. There are other developments in Gloucester and Berkshire. For further information tel: 01425 481225, visit www.archstone.co.uk or contact Annette Donovan, tel: 01425 481224.

CONTINUING CARE RETIREMENT COMMUNITY (CCRC)

The definition of a CCRC, is 'a planned purpose built living arrangement, which aims to meet the housing and personal needs of older people on one site'. These generally take the shape of either flats or bungalows and community buildings, as well as a community centre, nursing and residential care facilities. The idea being that those who need extra help, such as 24-hour nursing care, are catered for whilst independent living is also provided. Respite care or home care are provided should it be necessary. CCRC communities are well established in the US and they are also very popular in Germany.

ARE CCRC'S SELF FUNDING?

Most of the CCRC's in the US and Germany are not necessarily profit making. It is more likely that the schemes are sponsored by large organisations and charitable trusts such as The Red Cross. In the US these communities can be linked to religious denominations. These organisations provide the initial capital for the communities and residents pay the remainder through entrance fees and monthly payments. These payments are off-set against the original capital outlay and the running costs. The idea being that these communities will ultimately be self funding.

WHY ARE CCRC'S OPENING IN THE UK?

The 'grey' population in the UK is expected to increase annually with more strain put on social services. A study suggested that the UK population of those over the age of 65 will rise during the period of 2001–31 from 14% to 20%. It will be necessary to provide accommodation for the elderly who fall between two categories, being neither rich nor poor. Care resources for the elderly who have some financial means have been lacking, with those in need being expected to pay for their own provisions, as their savings can exclude them from some social services. At the same time, this group of people cannot afford to live solely on savings indefinitely, so technically they fall between two stools and as such CCRS's would appear to offer an economic solution to those who fall into this category. The downside of this is, of course, that some capital outlay would be necessary as an entry requirement to a CCRC.

Case study: A Lifetime Home at 'Hartrigg Oaks'

'Hartrigg Oaks' is two miles from the city centre of York and is the first CCRC to open in the UK. It is for people aged 60 plus. The accommodation is spread over a 21 acre site with landscaped gardens. It consists of 152 spacious one and two bedroom bungalows and 42 en-suite bed/sitting rooms situated within The Oaks Care Centre. Some bungalows have additional space in the roof, which can double up as a bedroom/office. Each bungalow has an easy maintenance garden plot and 24-hour CCTV to provide enhanced security to the site.

What facilities does it offer?

- Large licensed restaurant with waiter service
- Coffee shop
- Community shop
- Hairdressers
- Music room
- Health activity centre and spa
- Library
- Equipped computer room with Internet access
- People carrier

In addition to these facilities, there are various residents' groups and activities which are advertised on a communal notice board.

Are there any entry requirements?

There are certain entry requirements and Hartrigg Oaks prefers to take people in their 60s or 70s. The younger the applicant, the more of a chance they have of getting in, as the development is generally full and you will have to be placed on a 'reserve list'. Applicants must also pass a Health and Care Check and a Financial Assessment. Couples are given priority for the bungalows.

What are the costs involved in living there?

The residents make two contributions to the community's costs:

- Residence fee: this covers the occupation of a bungalow and, when required, a room in The Oaks. There are three options for payment of the residence fee.
  - A one-off fee: a single payment on joining. This is refundable and the full sum is repaid within two weeks of leaving.
  - Lower one-off fee: this is not refundable unless the resident leaves within a 56 month period, in which case a partial payment will be made.
  - Annualised fee: this is paid on a monthly basis and is not refundable.
- Community fee: this covers the cost of communal facilities: maintenance, landscaping, care support whether for a bungalow or The Oaks. There are three ways of making this payment.
  - Standard fee: this is an annual sum paid monthly. This payment does not vary according to the amount of care you need and is based on the age you were when joining.
  - Reduced fee: a lump sum payment which can reduce the standard fee by up to 50%.
  - Fee for care: a lower annual service charge. Care services are paid for only if required.

The community fee is reduced by 125% for couples. The Trust also guarantees that the community fee will not be increased in any one year more than 3% above the increase in the Retail Price Index (RPI) over the previous twelve months. The development is financially self-contained and fees will only change in line with the community's costs.

SUMMARY

There are many retirement schemes available across the UK and I would strongly advise visiting several before making any commitment. Also consider when you are doing your sums how much you currently spend on house maintenance, laundry, gardening, window cleaning and building insurance amongst other things. You may be surprised to discover the service charge might not be as onerous as you first thought.

My mother recently moved into a retirement apartment and we are both delighted with it. It offers help should she need it, companionship should she want it and above all . . . it allows her to maintain her independence. It is everything she could wish for.

If you choose not to live within a retirement scheme and wish to live completely independently without any back-up, you can source and purchase your retirement home in the traditional way, through an estate agent, internet or newspaper. Just remember, when making your choices, that if you choose a townhouse with lots of stairs, or somewhere isolated, or a house that's too big, you may find as you get less mobile that this is no longer suitable. So it is worth considering issues such as these before making your purchase, particularly if you don't want to have to move again.

No one can predict what future needs an individual may have, but it is almost certain that as a person ages, they become less mobile. So it is wise to bear this in mind when looking for a 'hassle free' retirement home. This does not mean to say that you have to compromise on what you want . . . it's just a question of thinking that bit further ahead.

Travel in Retirement

Do you want to see South America, the Panama Canal, Tahiti, Australia, New Zealand, Asia or Africa to name but a few places of interest? If you do, it is worth bearing in mind that retirement accounts for 20% of the average adult's life span (due to the increase in life expectancy) and retirees are spending this windfall of free time by packing their bags and heading for adventure. They are travelling the open road, flying the friendly skies and cruising the high seas. In fact, retirees account for nearly 40% of all package tours and one-third of all air travel and hotel stays.

Some of the reasons that travel is so desirable in retirement is because it removes you from the home environment and affords you the opportunity of meeting new people, some of whom may become friends. It allows you to experience different lifestyles, cultures and to learn new things. So, make the most of travel opportunities in retirement whilst you still can because the chances are if you don't travel now, you never will. So get your passport out and prepare to explore the wonders of the world. It's a great way to 'Spend The Kids' Inheritance'!

A FEW TRAVEL TIPS FOR RETIREES

Make sure you allow yourself enough time and money to see everything on offer. Explore the landscape, lifestyles and culture of your travels and keep an open, patient and inquisitive mind. Exercise before your travels as this will help you to have the stamina to explore all the sights. You should always wear comfortable clothing and carry an extra pair of glasses or contact lenses. Stick to your dietary routine as much as possible and don't forget any medication you might need. Arrange with a friend or relative to keep an eye on things at home and carry two home contact numbers with you at all times in case of an emergency. Most importantly, don't forget to have a good time!

MONEY

You don't necessarily need a great deal of money to travel, but you do need some. You can, of course, fly first class, stay in the best hotels, dine at the best restaurants and live the life of a millionaire – but only if you are one. Most of us have limited budgets and, although this does not mean you have to be prepared to backpack around the globe, you will have to watch what you spend and travel within the constraints of your budget.

You may not want to do all of your travelling in one hit, or even venture too far out of Europe, but if you want to and it is within your means then the world is your oyster.

VERY LIMITED BUDGET

For those on a very limited budget there are ways of doing swaps, a bit like the French Exchange Student schemes, where a French student comes over to live in the UK with a host family, in exchange for a reciprocal visit for an English student visiting France. www.globalfreeloaders.com is an on-line community, bringing people together to offer you free accommodation all over the world, helping you save money and make new friends, whilst seeing the world from a local's perspective! This only works, however, if you are prepared to offer your home in exchange. It does not necessarily mean that you have to offer three meals a day, just that you have to be prepared to offer what you yourself have received . . . quid pro quo as they say!

HOME EXCHANGE

This works on a similar basis to the above. Home exchange schemes allow you to make use of someone else's home whilst they, in exchange, are using yours. This can have advantages in that you will not incur the costs of staying in accommodation at your chosen location. You will also have someone else looking after your house whilst you are away. It is important, therefore, to do stringent reference checks, to ascertain that the person you are exchanging with will respect your home. Of course, there are no guarantees that they will and you must insist on seeing comprehensive images of the proposed exchange home. The chances are that if they do not look after their own house well, they are unlikely to look after yours. It is also recommended that you get in regular contact with the people you are planning to exchange with, either by phone, letter or e-mail. That way you can hopefully get a 'feel' for the person and gut instincts can often be your best bet in insuring against problems. Other facts to consider are:

- How big is your home and is it on parity with the exchange home?
- What are the ground rules regarding cleaning arrangements?

- Insurance, in case the trip is cancelled by either party.
- Ensuring that your visitors have ample space to store their clothes.
- Securing personal belongings.
- Informing the neighbours.
- Arrangements regarding bill payments (who will pay for what).
- Leave information about 'how the house works' and emergency contact numbers.
- Drawing up a contract.

Tel: 01962 886882 or visit www.homelink.org.uk and on request they will provide you with an information pack that covers all aspects of 'exchanging homes'. The website also allows you to view other properties that are offering exchange. A good US website to visit is www.HomeExchange.com or tel: +310 798 3864.

RETIRING

If you are considering retiring to a new area, travelling could be the perfect way of trying out a place before deciding to move there. Especially if you are considering retiring overseas.

DISCOUNT HOTEL DEALS

There are many ways of sourcing holiday deals and many hotels are only too happy to offer discounts when they are not busy. There are great deals to be had on city hotels, especially when the majority of their trade is business based, leaving the hotel virtually empty at weekends. You can often get deals such as three nights for the price of two at four and five star hotels, or heavily discounted rooms at most inner city locations. Try www.lastminute.com, (no landline number but you can get a useful link on your mobile phone by texting Mobile to 85959 which gets you on to the site). Another good site is Expedia: tel: 0870 050 0808 or visit www.expedia.co.uk to see what city break deals they are offering. City breaks are also advertised in newspapers and magazines, try the sunday supplements to see what offers are available. There is also www.ase.net. This search engine allows you to search the web for discount hotels, last minute hotel bookings, B&Bs and holiday rental accommodation anywhere in the world. The range is extensive, with over 220,000 web pages describing more than 150,000 individual properties. All you have to do is select your choice of location and price range, choose what amenities and facilities you require and the search engine does the rest. There is also a language option enabling you to select the language and currency of your choice.

CITY BREAKS

Whilst researching this book I decided to visit Paris and Berlin. Paris was booked via a Sunday newspaper offer which allowed me to stay two nights in a four star hotel in the centre of Paris for the price of one night. This included travel on Eurostar and breakfast at the hotel. The only downside to this deal was that I had to be prepared to travel at non-peak time, which resulted in having to leave Paris early Sunday morning.

When I visited Berlin I used a website and this deal included three nights for the price of two in a five star hotel in the centre of Berlin. The downside to this trip is that we assumed that breakfast at the hotel was included in the deal. This turned out not to be the case. So make sure you check when booking on the Internet exactly what is included and what isn't . . . otherwise you may end up with a big bill for your breakfast (as we did)!

UNIVERSITY ACCOMMODATION

Universities can be keen to rent out rooms affiliated with the university during the summer months. My mother used to visit York and stay at the halls of residence with the Towns Womens' Guild. This enabled them to stay in the centre of York without having to pay peak season hotel rates.

For details tel: 0114 249 3090 or visit www.venuemasters.com. They will send you a brochure of the facilities they have on offer and what price you can expect to pay. Most of the rooms enjoy en-suite facilities, so dismiss that dated image of student accommodation that you may have from your own student days!

TRAVELLING ALONE

To some this may seem like a daunting proposition, particularly if you have enjoyed travelling with a partner in the past. It does not, however, have to be the end of travelling if you are alone. Again, the Internet is the best place to explore your options. Visit www.solotourist.com. This site offers information on travelling alone. Some points to consider are:

- You are more likely to meet new people as you will be more approachable.
- You decide everything to do with your trip, from where you eat to how you spend the day.

A useful website to try is www.companions2travel.co.uk or tel: 0870 242 2335. This is an on-line community, where like-minded people can search out travelling companions from around the world. It assists you in linking up with someone else to help avoid single supplement payments and all the other aspects related to travelling alone. Another good website is www.friendshiptravel.com or tel: 0289 446 2211. They specialise in holidays for single travellers. They also offer Christmas breaks specifically catered to the needs of single people, where you can be with others in a similar situation. Although you are in a group, you can also spend time on your own. The advantage of this type of travel is that it is a bit like a halfway house if you feel that you do not want to totally go it alone. It is also a great opportunity for making new friends.

TAKING A GAP YEAR

Maybe when you enjoyed your student days or you were just plain young, the 'gap year' option did not exist in the same way as it does today. Certainly when I was at school, I didn't know of anyone who went on a gap year. Today, taking a gap year before going to university or college is considered the norm. So if you missed out on the gap year opportunities of your youth, you can make up for it now by doing a 'Gap Year for Grown Ups'. This is a chance to experience the gap year your children had. 'Gap year for grown ups' claims to provide meaningful travel opportunities all over the world. You can visit far-flung places, trek through mountains, explore tropical jungles, work with endangered animals and make a difference to people's lives in the world's poorest countries. Your trip can take two months or two years, it's up to you. Tel: 01892 701881 or visit www.gapyearforgrownups.co.uk.

SO YOU WANT TO GO ON A CRUISE?

One of the bonuses about being retired is that you can travel whenever you want and pick up the best deals. You are no longer required to fit in with work or term times. Going on a cruise can be a great way of enjoying a holiday, visiting various resorts with the entire organisation having been done for you and it doesn't have to be expensive. It is also a great way to meet people and if you are on your own and don't feel up to looking around the sights, then you can stay on board and enjoy the facilities.

Cruise advice for the 'first timer'

Those who have travelled on a cruise before recommend getting to the embarkation point a day early. This way, if there are any last minute travel delays, you won't be caught up in them. This will help in achieving a relaxing start to the holiday rather than a stressed out one. Cheap deals can always be found on the Internet for hotel rooms. So do your research and chill out in a nice hotel before the 'big day'. Other things to consider are:

◆ Check out what excursions are on offer and book early to avoid any disappointment.

◆ If you want to book any hair appointments or beauty treatments then make sure you do it early, as these appointments are the first to go. Similarly if the ship has an à la carte/alternative restaurant, you will need to book in advance.

◆ Hire cars can be expensive if booked through the cruise line for off-shore trips. Plan car hire in advance and check out local companies for the best deals. The Internet is invaluable for this kind of research.

◆ Luxury ships have a DVD and video collection but the best of the selection will go early. If there is something you really want to watch, get in early (but make sure you return it as soon as you have watched it).

◆ If you have a noisy neighbour or a problem with the cabin, inform the Purser immediately and they will do their best to sort out the problem. It is in their interests for you to be a happy passenger.

◆ If you are unhappy with whom you are sharing a dining table, speak to the maître d' and ask to be assigned to another table.

◆ If you purchase an air/sea package it will be the cruise line's responsibility to track down your luggage should it go astray.

◆ If you purchase an air/sea package ensure that they are offering you a direct route. If not, contact the cruise line's air deviation desk and for a small fee they may be able to help you.

◆ Pack a small bag with a change of clothes and some toiletries to keep with you as hand baggage. Your luggage may take some time to arrive at your cabin and possibly not arrrive in time for you to change before dinner.

What can I expect when I arrive at the embarkation point?

◆ You will hand your luggage to the porter who will put it in 'bins' and deliver it to your cabin later.

◆ In the terminal building you will go through the same security procedure as at an airport.

- At the check-in desk you will register and provide proof of identification and a credit card. Once this is done, you'll be given your 'shipboard charge card'. This serves as ID and you will be able to use this card on board for any purchases. In some cases, the same card acts as the key to your cabin.

- The next step depends on your arrival time at the pier. If you're at the pier before they've begun boarding the ship, you'll be given a number or letter and be asked to wait in an embarkation lounge until your number/letter is called for boarding. If you arrive after initial boarding has started, you'll just follow the signs to the gangway.

- Walking on board, you'll be greeted by cruise line personnel. You may be given a map of where to locate your cabin or alternatively an attendant will take you there.

- Don't be surprised by the size of your cabin as it is most likely going to be very small. The upside to living in a box is that there is less space to 'roll' in inclement weather conditions! Further inspection of the cabin will most likely reveal that you have everything you need, particularly in the way of storage.

- You will be introduced to your cabin steward (a few 'tips' here and there will not go amiss).

- You will be given information about your assigned dining room.

- Dinner will not be until the evening, but there should be a buffet lunch laid on. Do not expect too much of the food or you could be disappointed.

- Remember that you will be expected to pay for all drinks, even though those welcome drinks with umbrellas look like a freebie! You will be asked for your charge card to purchase all beverages.

- Get to know the ship, have a good walk about and most importantly memorise where your cabin is!

- There will be a lifeboat drill and after that a 'sail away party'.

- After dinner there will be various entertainment options from cabaret to casino to ballroom dancing. Or even a romantic stroll on deck in the moonlight!
- Before you retire, check out what the ship has on offer the next day as you don't want to miss out on anything. Bon voyage!

FOR THE WOMAN TRAVELLING ALONE

There are some organisations which cater exclusively for women travelling alone. For those who are used to travelling with a partner, 'going it alone' can be unfamiliar, so it is comforting to know that you can travel with others who are in a similar situation. Visit www.thelmandlouise.com. This is a company run by Christine Davies and Grace Frankel who have been friends for twenty years. Both have had families, but now find themselves alone. Their website states that they share their talents and professional experience and run a women only travel club. This enables women to find a travel buddy through a protective network, so that they can plan to fulfil their travel aspirations with the security of like minded companionship.

Walking in Spain

Butterfly Adventures are a husband and wife team. They offer three types of holiday for women who travel alone or with friends, and who enjoy walking, being in the countryside and sightseeing. There are three holidays on their website to choose from:

- Walks in Alto Genal – combining gentle walking with free time to either relax or choose from the different activities on offer.
- Andalusian cultural walks – combining culture with gentle walking.
- Total relaxation – combining massage with gentle walking to unwind totally.

To contact Butterfly Adventures tel: +34 952 180 763 or visit www. butterflyadventures.co.uk.

TRAVELLING WITH A DISABILITY

Accessible Travel are a company specialising in arranging holidays for people with disabilities. Their aim is to take care of all of your holiday arrangements from start to finish. They will organise wheelchair access and any special needs and can offer advice on equipment hire and travelling overseas with a wheelchair. They will send you a brochure on request, detailing all the holidays available. They can be contacted on tel: 01452 729 739 or visit www.accessibletravel.co.uk.

THE OLDER TRAVELLER

Tour companies that cater to the more mature traveller offer holidays at a slower pace, rather than cramming as many activities in as possible. For more information contact Grand UK Holidays, tel: 01603 886700 or visit www.grandukholidays.com. Their website is aimed specifically at people over 55 who are travelling alone, with friends or a partner. There are many holiday destinations to choose from throughout Britain, Europe and beyond. The accommodation choices range from four star luxury, to friendly family run hotels. There are scenic coach tours, traditional Christmas holidays, cruises to exotic countries, weekends away and special winter sun holidays in the Mediterranean. Contact them by e-mail and request a brochure for all the latest holiday offers.

Vegetarians can also be catered for when making travel choices. Contact: www.vegetarianuk.com.

FOR THE ADVENTUROUS

If you want to try a holiday that is going to be more adventure based visit www.eldertreks.com. This is an organisation run exclusively for the over 50s. They claim to offer you a unique travel experience by taking you off the beaten track. Eldertreks promote the fact that they do not offer rigidly planned itineraries, but encourage spontaneity to give a unique travel experience. If you are willing to share a room, there are no single supplements and they welcome the 'lone' traveller. Their trips claim to explore the culture and nature of a destination. The travelling groups are kept small with no more than 15 people in a group. All trips involve walking and some include hiking in rainforest, desert or mountain environments. So, if you do not enjoy a modicum of fitness, this type of holiday will not be for you!

EXOTIC TRAVEL

Maybe there is somewhere you have always wanted to visit and never got round to it. The great advantage of retirement is that you can be very flexible about your travel arrangements and pick up the best deals. If you have always dreamed of visiting far away places and different cultures then retirement is the time to fulfil those dreams.

India

I travelled to Mumbai/Bombay a few months ago and I thought it was a most extraordinary place. India was like nothing I had ever seen before. India is a trip that should last for at least four weeks in order to do it justice. It is difficult to describe India as it is so diverse. Yes, there is poverty, corruption, degradation, but the place is teeming with life and energy . . . everyone trying to make a rupee where they can.

India is now becoming more accessible from the UK, as the number of flights has doubled, helping to keep prices low. There are many areas to visit from Delhi and the Taj Mahal to Goa, the temples of the south and the Himalayas. If you fancy the trip of a lifetime then India could be the place for you. For flights call Air India, tel: 020 8560 9996 or visit www.airindia.com or call Jet Airways, tel: 0870 607 0222 or visit www.jetairways.com. Charters serve Goa from Gatwick and Manchester, which tend to be cheaper. Call Charter Flights, tel: 0845 045 0153 or visit www.charterflights.co.uk.

Travelling in India

If you want to travel by air visit www.flykingfisher.com or tel: (India) +91 124 2844700/(UK) 1600 180 3333 or visit www.spicejet.com. Internal flights in India are not expensive, but if you fancy something different, travelling by train is a fantastic way of seeing India. It is quite slow, but that is the beauty of it. You can travel on overnight sleepers or on daytime expresses. To book tel: 0208 903 3411 or visit www.india rail.co.uk. If you want to travel in luxury and are prepared to pay the premium, tel: 01904 521900 or visit www.greatrail.com. Alternatively you can travel by car, if you are brave enough, or you can hire a driver for the day which is inexpensive and takes the hard work out of it. I tried it this way and it was a very pleasant day out from Mumbai to the Gateway of India, and further on a ferry to the Elephanta Isle. Try hiring a driver for the day through your hotel and as always, get a nominated price in advance. Plan when to go to India carefully and watch out for the monsoon season, generally from June to September!

Safari

I recently went on safari with my family to Kenya and we all thoroughly enjoyed it. The great thing about going 'on safari' is that it is a fantastic way of seeing wild animals roaming around their natural habitat and doing what they have to do to survive (which in a nutshell means eating other animals!). There are plenty of other animals to see as well as the 'big five' of lions, leopards, water buffalo, rhinos and elephants such as zebras, cheetahs and giraffes.

The beauty of safari is that you do not have to enjoy great mobility to get the best out of the holiday as very little walking is involved. You stay on the mini bus mainly (if you didn't you might get eaten by a lion!) and are taken on 'game drives'. There are on average three game drives a day and you are guaranteed to see and get close to many animals. It is important that you take binoculars with you and be prepared to be on the bus for long hours, as the distance from one game reserve to another can be quite considerable. Another point to remember is that the roads in Kenya and most of East Africa are not good, so the journeys can be very rough and bumpy. If you have back problems or don't enjoy being driven around in a mini bus, then this may not be the holiday for you. If you do not mind sitting on a mini bus or jeep and seeing the wonders of Africa unfold before your eyes, you will have the most fantastic holiday. Everyone I spoke to on safari was delighted with the holiday and wanted to do it again. It is important to be aware however of when the animals migrate and when the rains come, as Africa, believe it or not, can be quite cold at times, particularly in the early mornings and evenings.

For accommodation we stayed in lodges which are well equipped and clean (although the standard can vary from lodge to lodge, as does the price). The best lodge we stayed in was one of the Serena chain, which have a reputation (deservedly) for being the best lodges. The more adventurous traveller can stay under canvas and this is apparently a wonderful experience. The tents are much more luxurious than the ones you put up in the back garden for the kids to play in!

Going on safari can be quite hard work as you will have to get up early to enjoy some of the game drives. You may also have to leave early to travel to the next lodge. So having a few days to unwind at the end of your holiday in a beach hotel is well worth it, even if it is a plane trip away. We spent four days in Mombasa relaxing by the pool and it was a great way to end the best holiday we have ever had! There are many companies that offer 'The Safari Experience' but we went with Trailfinders, tel: 0845 058 5858 or visit www.trailfinders.com for further information.

SKI HOLIDAYS

Not to be confused with 'Spending the Kids' Inheritance'! There are literally hundreds of ski holidays available, from self-catering to staying in hotels and chalets. Snowboarding is also very popular. Some of the companies specialising in skiing are: Ski-Ski-Ski, tel: 0808 1089 100 or visit www.ski-ski-ski.co.uk. Also, Ski1st: tel: 0870 421 1955 or www.ski1st.co.uk. For on-line deals see www.teletextski.co.uk.

SUMMARY

Whatever you decide to do in retirement, travel should be part of the game plan. So all that remains to be said is . . . bon voyage!

TRAVELLING CLOSER TO HOME
Driving

When you reach your 70th birthday you will have to renew your driving licence and continue to do this every three years. If you have developed a medical condition you will have to declare it on the renewal application form that you should receive automatically. You may then be required to have a medical examination on the advice of your doctor. If you just enjoy driving and wish to improve your skills and get an honest assessment of your ability, there are various courses open to you. They may not appeal to the 'boy racer' in you, and you may find that you are more 'rusty' than you think and will enjoy the time learning to improve. It will also help with your confidence on the road, particularly if you are awarded a 'Gold Pass' or the equivalent. For further information see:

◆ The Royal Society for the Prevention of Accidents (RoSPA) Experienced Driver Assessment on tel: 0121 248 2000 or visit www.rospa.org.uk.
◆ The RoSPA advanced driving test on tel: 0870 777 2099 or visit www.roada.org.uk.
◆ The Institute of Advanced Motoring (IAM) Advanced Driving Test on tel: 0208 996 9600 or visit www.iam.org.uk.

◆ The IAM skill for life package which includes a driving course, the test, a manual and a year's membership to the IAM (see above for details).

Driving with disabilities

Mobility centres can advise older people with disabilities on all aspects of driving. They will assess your disability and advise you about any adaptations or equipment you would need in order to drive. The charity 'Ricability', tel: 0207 427 2460 or www.ricability.org.uk, produces leaflets to assist on:

◆ car controls
◆ people lifters
◆ getting a wheelchair into a car.

GETTING AROUND BY TRAIN

If you are intending to travel by train then a senior railcard would be well worth the investment. For an initial outlay (it is currently £20) you will be able to travel (non-peak) for two thirds of the price of most fares in the UK (including saver tickets). You can pick up an application form at your local station or contact National Rail Enquiries, tel: 08457 48 49 50, for more information. There are also other types of cheap fare tickets which generally require you to book in advance. Check with enquiries for the best deals. At weekends you can travel first class on a saver ticket, if you pay a small supplement (currently £10) you will get complimentary coffee/tea/biscuits. So if you are planning on drinking a few cups this could be a saving!

Getting around by train with a disability

All train companies and Network Rail have agreed a code of practice to assist disabled travellers. If you think you are going to need assistance, call the train company beforehand and give them at least 24 hours' notice where possible. The disabled railcard offers similar discounts to the senior railcard, but is cheaper and allows you to take a companion with you at the reduced rate. For more information on rail travel for disabled passengers, tel: 08457 48 49 50 or visit www.disabledpersons-railcard.co.uk.

Train travel abroad

If you purchase a 'rail-card Plus', on top of your senior railcard, this will allow you to travel for 25% less on most trains in Europe. Tel: 08705 848848 for details. Eurostar does not subscribe to the scheme, but offer their own independent deals for people aged 60 plus and for those with disabilities, tel: 08705 186186 or visit www.eurostar.com.

Rail Europe

Rail Europe also sells 'French Railways Carte Senior' which gives discounts of up to 50% on French trains, depending on availability, visit www.raileurope.com.

COACH TRAVEL

You can get an Advantage 50 Discount coach card which is available to anyone over 50 and gives discounts of up to 30% on standard fares. Contact the National Express coach station by calling: 08705 898989 or visit www.national-coach-travel.co.uk.

Coach travel with a disability

As from January 2005 all new coaches must be wheelchair friendly, but it will take time for the old stock to be phased out. If you think you may need help contact the National Express Additional Needs helpline, tel: 0121 423 8479.

BUSES

Everyone over 60 is entitled to a free bus pass in Scotland, Wales and most parts of England. Some bus passes in England, depending on the area, only allow a 50% reduction in fares, but from April 2006 you may be entitled to free off-peak travel on your local bus services if you're disabled or aged 60 plus. In Northern Ireland bus travel is free for those 65 plus.

Bus travel with a disability

New buses have had to be wheelchair friendly since the year 2000 but, as with the coaches, it will be some time before existing stock is phased out. All buses have designated seats for the disabled. Contact your local bus company for further information.

DIAL-A-RIDE SCHEMES

To find out what schemes are operating in your area, contact your local authority, the Community Transport Association or your local Citizens Advice Bureau (CAB) office.

TAKE A CAB

If you can afford it . . . why not? You could even set up an account with a local cab company, just make sure they are licensed. There are also taxi card schemes operating in some areas offering low cost taxis, but check with your local authority.

Shopping mobility

Some shopping centres loan out wheelchairs to the elderly or disabled so that they can shop independently. Check with your shopping centre to see what facilities they provide for the shopper with mobility problems or call: 08456 442 446 or visit www.justmobility.co.uk.

Scooters and buggies

If you have mobility problems you can get advice from the Disabled Living Foundation on tel: 0845 130 9177 or visit www.dlf.org.uk, your nearest disabled living centre or the Mobility Information Service. They will all offer advice on what type of scooter or buggy you should be looking for and what special features you might find useful. You can also call Tripscope, tel: 08457 585641 or visit www.tripscope.org.uk, which offers advice on disabled travel facilities at home and abroad.

SUMMARY

It's important to get out and about if you want to remain active and have a social life. Make the most of transport opportunities in your area particularly as most senior travel is heavily discounted . . . you might as well take advantage!

4

Hobbies and Learning

A new hobby can bring with it much pleasure, satisfaction and can help keep you active in retirement. The alternative is to do nothing and get rusty, not only physically, but mentally. If you are going to keep your faculties, you are going to have to use them. The point of retirement is that you can choose to do things because you want to do them, and not because you have to do them to satisfy work commitments or other people. Obviously, retiring on an unlimited budget makes anything possible, as does good health but even if you are not rich in either, there is no reason why you shouldn't enjoy your life to the full. You may have to adapt your dreams but there is no need to give up on them . . . not unless you want to be bored to death!

LEARNING SOMETHING NEW

You may still link the thought of learning something new to your school days, when learning was most likely a chore that you did not relish. Learning doesn't have to be like that and it can be great fun, particularly if you are learning about something that interests you. Learning can also be a way of doing something you enjoy, alongside other like-minded people in a relaxed environment. Learning for leisure can also build your confidence and act as a stepping-stone back into more academic studies. You can take courses in just about anything you want, anywhere from colleges and learning centres to libraries and outdoor locations. You can learn over a weekend, do a full university course or even go on a learning holiday. Here are just a few examples of the huge range of creative and practical courses available.

Computer skills

It's impossible to ignore the significance of computers and the Internet. If you want to get the most out of your retirement, you simply have to 'get on-line'. That way you will be able to source the best holidays, courses, deals and explore a world of opportunities. It is most definitely a major disadvantage if you are not 'connected' to the Internet. If you are one of those people who feel that you are too old to learn new tricks or that using a computer will be too technical for you to master, ditch those feelings right now! It's much simpler than you think and the Internet is arguably the most exciting, powerful tool of modern times. So, why stand by and say things like . . . 'I don't do e-mail', 'I haven't got a computer' or 'I don't know anything about the Internet' when you can learn. You've got the time and there's every reason why you should learn. Without it you are quite simply going to be left behind and miss out on a modern marvel. So, enter the new world and contact your local council offices, Citizens Advice Bureau or library to find out what courses are available in your area. Or get someone you know with Internet access to look on the 'web' for you. Don't delay! Get connected today and the world will be quite literally at your finger tips.

The Open University (OU)

If you want to 'distance learn' a subject with the view to obtaining a degree, The Open University has many courses to choose from. Its website states:

> The Open University is the UK's only university dedicated to distance learning. For most courses there are no previous qualifications required to study and there is no upper age limit. We have around 150,000 undergraduate and more than 30,000 postgraduate students. 10,000 of our students have disabilities. The Open University's style of teaching is called 'supported open learning'. Nearly all students are studying part-time. About 70% of undergraduate students are in full-time employment. More than 50,000 students are sponsored by their employers for their studies. 11,000 people are currently studying for OU Higher Degrees. Most OU courses are available throughout Europe. Some of them are available in many other parts of the world. More than 25,000 OU students live outside the UK. The University itself is ranked among the top UK universities for the quality of its teaching. A third of UK undergraduate students have entry qualifications lower than those normally demanded by other UK universities.

For further information tel: 01908 274066 or visit www.3.open.ac.uk/courses.

Genealogy

If you have always wanted to find out more about your past, now is the time to try. Genealogy is the study of families and their ancestors. If you are a beginner, you can start by visiting your local library and doing some research. There are many useful introductory books on genealogy and family history which will provide you with advice on how to get started. Another way to begin is to contact all your family members. Check with them to find out what documents (certificates, letters, newspaper cuttings, photograph albums, diaries, etc.) they have in their possesion. Try to establish, as completely as possible, the basic genealogical facts (date and place of birth, date and place of marriage, and date and place of death/burial) of as many of your near relatives as you can. Useful websites are www.ancestory.co.uk or www.britishgeneolgy.com.

Cookery

Learning how to cook can be fun and challenging. Whether you are a complete cookery beginner or are looking to enrol onto a gourmet master class, you will be able to find a course that's right for you. If you are considering learning more about cooking, be it vegetarian, Chinese, Italian or Indian, there are many recipe books and cookery programmes to get you started. If you are looking for a course, try visiting www.directgov.co.uk or contact your local council for further information.

Cookery holidays

If you want to combine a cookery course with a holiday, try Holiday on the Menu; tel: 08708 998844 or visit www.holidayonthemenu.com. In their marketing, they offer:

To find you opportunities to learn to cook in spectacular locations. From India to Indonesia, Morocco to Mexico, or Sydney to Seville. Our teachers range from gourmet chefs to local women who have been cooking almost since they could walk. Classes are intimate and deliberately small, to allow for plenty of individual attention. You work with fantastic fresh produce, cooking authentic regional food. Always there are fascinating market trips with your chef. Often, you get to pick ingredients from the local farms or gardens. What better way to learn about a country than through its food and flavours, choosing vegetables at the markets, sharing stories over a bubbling pot. None require you to be an expert cook, the courses are for the enthusiast, not the professional chef and the atmosphere is relaxed, educational and fun.

Check on the Internet for other holiday cookery courses as there are many to choose from.

Gardening

Retirement is almost synonomous with gardening and the image of the elderly in their potting sheds or pruning their roses is one which we are all familiar with. Today, there are different types of gardening to choose from and there are widespread courses available, ranging from organic gardening, to landscaping, to installing a water feature, to basic gardening or, for the more ambitious, garden design.

♦ Organic gardening: this type of gardening uses substantial diversity in pest control to reduce the use of pesticides and tries to provide fertility with local sources of nutrients rather than purchased fertilisers. To find out more tel: 01896 860661 or visit www.learning-curve.org. For a fee you can do a course from home and their study topics include: History of the Organic Movement; Organic Gardening and the Environment; Soil Cultivation and Management; Organic Cultivation of Fruit and Vegetable Crops; The Herb Garden; An Organic Diet; Accreditation of Organic Crops; Greenhouse Gardening; Controlling Pests and Diseases; Weed Control; Conservation and the Gardener; Encouraging Wildlife; The Garden Pond and Planning your Organic Garden.

♦ Landscaping: this is a skill that, as well being a hobby, is something that could earn you an income in retirement. It may be that you are semi-retired and have given up the 'day job' in order to pursue your passion for gardening. You may be able to find an adult education course through your local authority or you may choose a 'distance learning' course where a fee will be payable. To find out more tel: 0207 6812702 or visit www.acsedu.co.uk to look at their correspondence course which covers all areas, such as horticultural practices, management, plant identification, plant use and marketing.

◆ Water garden features: If you want to do a course on-line then you should visit www.universalclass.com/agriculture. They offer a course which, 'will outline how to design and build a garden pond, waterfall, fountain, gazebo, tub garden, or other structure'. It also offers information on the types of plants suitable for various situations. It is the ideal course for those who want to improve their garden and provides ideas and tips to help transform a plain yard into the garden of your dreams. Three basic possibilities exist for the home garden pond: a small accent pool, a formal pool or a natural pool. Available materials range from the more traditional stone, brick and concrete to ready-made liners and shells. In addition there are pumps, filters, lights and other accoutrements that can be incorporated into your dream pond.

Home improvement

Home improvement can cover a multitude of sins, some of which are covered in other chapters. There are many areas of home improvement which will enhance a property and add to its value. The courses concentrated on here cover cosmetic rather than structural improvements. For a weekend break/course tel: 00 34 962 703 231 or visit www.press dispensary.co.uk. You should also try www.thecourselocator.co.uk for information on other courses.

◆ Feng shui or fengshui, translated from Chinese, means wind and water. It is the ancient Chinese practice of placement and arrangement of space to achieve harmony with the environment. It has its origins in 'Taoism' and is estimated to be more than three thousand years old. For information on courses available tel: 0208 332 7588 or visit www.fengshuibritain.co.uk.

- Soft furnishings: using fabric to give rooms an instant facelift by adding curtains, cushions, tablecloths and covers to windows, sofas, tables and beds. Courses can teach you how to use fabrics, in different colours, textures and patterns. Visit www.hutchal.clara.net for some free tips and advice. Tel: 023 805 79282 for information on alternative windows.
- DIY can range from painting and decorating to plumbing, building, putting up shelves amongst others things. There are many courses available to help you if you want to learn the basics and these courses cover a range of subjects from carpentry to plastering. Visit www.directgov.uk, contact your local council or tel: 0800 389 4080 or visit www.thecourselocator.co.uk. For general information and advice tel: 0845 061 8899 or visit www.igoe.ie.

Learning a language

If you want to learn another language there are hundreds of courses available across the country. Whether you are a complete beginner or at a more advanced level, there will be a course for you. If you are considering a move overseas in retirement, being able to speak the language (or at least some of it) will be a great advantage. Some of the languages you could learn include:

- French
- Spanish
- Italian
- Dutch
- German
- Russian
- Japanese
- Chinese

There are many language courses available, far too numerous to mention here, but as an example if you want to learn from a book, CD or CD Rom then phone: 0800 136973 or visit www.linguaphone.co.uk. You can also learn a language on-line at www.edufind.com and if you want to study a language in the country itself, visit www.learn-languages-abroad.co.uk.

Art

Exploring your artistic side can be a great way of learning a new skill. You do not have to be a budding 'Rembrandt' to enjoy art classes. As art classes are often taken in groups with one student often learning from another, they can also be a great way of making new friends. There are many different courses available, from beginners to advanced and the courses covered range from learning how to paint in watercolour or oil, to life drawings and paintings, sculpture and calligraphy. There are also courses available in learning the History of Art where you can visit museums and art galleries, discuss individual painters, their techniques and the role they played as artists during the time and place in which they lived.

Developing skills in art

If you enjoy art, or want to develop your skills, you will be able to find a course where you can work at your own pace and at a time that suits you. There are many courses on offer such as The Tate On-line Courses. The Tate courses offer level one free and this is what they say about it:

Although the course is open to all, it is designed for people who might be new to modern or contemporary art, or new to learning in general. You may or may not have visited any one of the four Tate galleries. You may or may not have been to college to study art or any other subjects. In short, the course is for anyone, regardless of how much you know about art or about computers.

Visit www.tate.org.uk for more information.

There are many other art courses available. For example, visit www.directgov.uk or www.definitionzone.com for information on art schools and classes. If you want to combine learning art with a trip overseas, there are many 'art holidays' to choose from. Contact tel: 0800 458 9044 or visit www.paintinginitaly.com, tel: 01691 656 788 or visit www.artholidaysfrance.com or www.artcourses.co.uk.

If you wish to study art at a residential course within the UK, there are many to choose from. But if you fancy country house splendour tel: 01653 648 444, visit www.castlehoward.co.uk, tel: 015394 35280 or visit www.heatoncooper.co.uk.

Photography

Photography is about more than having a 'good eye', expensive equipment and being in the right place at the right time and, as a result of this, there are a wide range of courses on offer. There is something for everyone, regardless of whether you are a complete beginner, wanting to improve your photographic skills or an experienced photographer wanting to 'gen up' on the latest digital technology. As with all other hobbies, photography offers opportunities of meeting like-minded people who share the same interests as you and often new friendships can be formed. Try www.amateurphotography.com for news and course information. Visit www.icslearn.co.uk for City and Guilds home study courses. Contact: 0118 9017272 or visit www.thephotographyschool. co.uk for other courses.

Dance

Don't worry if you have two left feet, you can still learn to dance. Dancing is an enjoyable way for people of all ages to keep fit and meet new people in a relaxed environment. Currently, there are almost 4,000 different courses available, covering every style of dance. Below are some of the styles available.

Salsa

Salsa is the dance of the moment. As the music has spread around the world, various salsa styles have emerged including Cuban and Puerto Rican. All are based on the same rhythms, but with varying steps, body movements and turns. For those who are beginners to the world of dance, salsa is one of the more accessible forms of partner dance and is relatively easy to learn. Visit www.uksalsa.com for information on all aspects of salsa. Alternatively you can learn to Salsa from DVDs and videos, try www.activevideos.com or www.lets-dance-salsa.com. If you are looking for a salsa holiday tel: 0870 286 6000 or visit www.danceholidays.com.

Line dancing

Line dancing is normally done in a group and is great for people without partners. It is a series of steps performed by a group of dancers assembled in a line. It involves a variety of walking, kicking and turning movements done in unison to music. The dancers dance side by side, doing the same steps. Normally the dancers move around the floor facing different walls as they progress through the dance steps. It is not complicated and is great fun and can be enjoyed by anyone. There are new line dance steps emerging all the time, so there are always plenty of different dances to learn. Visit www.learntodance.com for information on line dancing in your area or www.dancelovers.com for DVD and video information.

Ballroom dancing

Ballroom dancing is back in fashion, with the success of 'Strictly Come Dancing' on TV giving it a new lease of life. It is estimated that more than one million people regularly go to ballroom dancing classes and those that don't, can learn to tango, waltz or foxtrot in the privacy of their own home with the help of dance videos and DVDs. Visit www.dancetv.com, www.ballroomdancers.com or www.dancesport.com. You can even go online to find a partner by visiting www.dancepartners.com.

Wine tasting courses

You may be interested in learning more about wine. If so, www.wine educators.com are a UK group of independent wine educators who run wine courses, wine tastings, seminars and holidays for both trade and consumers. Other courses can be found at tel: 0870 9004 300 or visit www.berrybrosandrudd.com, tel: 0207 261 5000 or visit www. decanter.com.

Wine tours

If you are really keen on wine, a holiday incorporating a wine tour could be just what you are looking for. Arblaster & Clarke Wine Tours was founded in 1986 by Tim Clarke and Lynette Arblaster. They share a passion for wine and a love of travelling. On their tours they offer wine guides who are:

> Friendly and approachable and appreciate that in a party there will be all levels of experience and interest. If you don't know much about a region, all the more reason to travel with a Wine Guide. The Wine Guide will make the region make sense, and put it in the context of other regions. The Wine Guide can give you the inside story, the gossip, the real history, the run down on the vintages, the producers and the wines and each guide is accompanied by a Tour Manager, who helps ensure that all runs smoothly and keeps your glass topped up!

Tel: 01730 893 344 or visit www.winetours.co.uk for further information. There are many other companies that offer wine holidays, which you will be able to find by 'surfing the net' or through your nearest wine appreciation society.

SUMMARY

There are so many courses available it would be impossible to list them all here. The ones listed above are just an example of what's on offer.

Basically if you want to learn about something, be it from making chocolate to candles, there will be a course available to teach you how to do it. Not all courses cost money and to find out what is available in your area, contact your local council or www.directgov.uk or visit www.britishinformation.com. Most courses are available at different levels so you can learn with people of similar ability to yourself. Courses can be solely for entertainment but some do offer qualifications . . . so go out, have fun, make new friends and learn something new today.

5

Retirement Overseas – Living the Dream

Have you ever dreamt of leaving the UK and its unpredictable climate for more sunny shores? 'Spending the Kids' Inheritance' sitting on your terrace by your pool, glass in hand, sunshine beating down on you, as you look out onto a panoramic view of the sea or some spectacular countryside? Well, if you haven't, many Britons have and those that are adventurous and believe in living the dream, rather than just dreaming it, have sold up and moved to sunnier shores. Retiring abroad is an increasingly viable option these days and all the evidence suggests that it will become even more so in the future. However, that dream can sometimes turn into a nightmare and, as with any move, it needs to be carefully thought out and planned for. Things to consider before packing up for good are listed below.

SPEAKING THE LANGUAGE

Moving to any country merits learning the language, no matter what age you are . . . it really is a case of it's never too late to learn. Being able to speak the native language is an enormous advantage and there are various ways to learn a language, through books, courses and evening classes. If it is your aim to retire overseas, the sooner you start to learn the language the better, even if it is years before the planned move. So start enrolling now! Further information on language courses can be found in Chapter 4 (Hobbies and Learning).

CLIMATE

Let's face it, we all get fed up with the British climate, but it is worth checking out that the country of your choice promises the sunshine that you hoped for as many warm climates can have surprisingly harsh winters.

CRIME

There is also a sense among some of the older generation that Britain is increasingly becoming a victim of 'yob culture'. A lot of town and city centres are becoming no-go areas at night-time for the elderly, who feel vulnerable and at risk. Moving overseas appears to offer a solution to this problem. But it can often turn out that far from living in the crime free haven they dreamt of, they are in fact being singled out as easy targets for the growing crime wave in other countries, particularly Spain.

LOVED ONES

It's important that you consider fully what impact being away from loved ones will have on your life. According to a study by Age Concern, almost half of all Britons who emigrate eventually move back home. This can be for all sorts of reasons, including being homesick for family and friends, financial and health reasons and missing the British way of life.

BEING LEFT ALONE IN A FOREIGN COUNTRY

No matter which country you choose to retire to, it is worth considering how you would feel if you were left there alone. Would you be able to cope being so far away from home and would you have the support that you would need? Would you want to return home to your family and friends and could you afford to do so? Obviously you may not want to think of these things but it would be unwise not to, particularly if you are buying a property that may prove difficult to sell because of market forces such as oversupply, lack of finances to facilitate a move, or property desirability.

OCCUPATION/HOBBIES

You may have hobbies and jobs that you may not be able to pursue overseas. Check whether you will be able to continue doing the things you enjoy in your free time and, if not, consider whether or not you will be happy adapting to new interests.

HEALTH

There is growing evidence of the benefits that a Mediterranean diet can bring and coupled with a more laid back lifestyle this will inevitably reduce stress levels. There are statistics that show heart disease is considerably lower in France, Spain, Italy and Greece than in the UK. However, you will need to consider carefully whether the climate will actually suit you, as what may be great for two weeks of the year could become uncomfortable for longer. It is also important that you consider the diet – especially if you are fond of English fare!

SELLING UP AND MOVING WHERE?

For those Britons selling medium range houses between £500,000 and £800,000, the most common destination is France or Spain – and more recently Dubai. For those with more cash in the coffers, their destinations can be as far away as New Zealand and the US, particularly Florida.

THE IMPACT ON THE BRITISH ECONOMY

Over 191,000 Britons reportedly emigrated last year alone and these tended to be the more affluent members of society. This means they are taking a lot of money out of the country with them and are no longer players in the British housing market. As a contrast, those entering the country last year, numbered around 150,000, tend to be poorer migrant workers from Eastern Europe who are unable, in the short-term, to get on the housing ladder. This obviously has a negative effect on the British economy as a whole. Particularly as in 1980 Exchange Controls were lifted, allowing Britons to take their wealth with them. Up to that time there were regulations in place preventing them from doing so. This has encouraged people to move abroad.

VIVA ESPANA

Sun . . . Sea . . . Sangria . . . what a great way to 'Spend The Kids' Inheritance'! For some, the Spanish way of life is living the dream. As Spain is part of the EU all you need to do if you have decided to retire there is apply for a resident's card within 90 days of moving there. You will need proof of ID, income and accommodation. You will also need to obtain a Fiscal Identity Number (NIF) from the local police station. Finding the property of your dreams, however, might prove a little harder and this is where you will need to have your wits about you in order to make the right purchase for the right price.

BUYING OFF PLAN IN SPAIN

As in the UK, property market buying off plan offers the opportunity of purchasing a property at a discount below market value. If you are not planning to retire for another couple of years, buying off plan may suit you well.

How it works

+ During the construction stage your property rises in value.
+ The earlier you purchase a property the greater your discount will be as the developer will be keen to 'kick start' his development and sell properties below market value.
+ The market value of each property can be compared with the price of similar properties with similar specifications in similar areas.
+ The more properties a developer sells, the more his financial obligations are met.
+ The first significant price increases will usually take place in the second phase of the development.
+ Remaining price increases occur periodically throughout the construction period.
+ The final phase is generally the most expensive phase.

Inspection trips

Many developers/companies offer inspection trips of their schemes, which generally last three to four days. The cost of the inspection trips vary and can be anything from £40 upwards. The price includes return flights and a stay in a three star hotel. Most companies who run such inspection trips claim that they will not use hard sell techniques, but you can be sure that they will do their best to sell you a property before you depart for home. These companies are not out to finance a short break for you in Spain, they want to sell you a property. That is their business and that is how they make their money. Once you have booked such a trip they will arrange everything for you, including flights, accommodation and, most importantly, a tour of the area in their air-conditioned mini buses to show you the properties on offer. Some companies offer one-to-one inspection trips but most will cater for two couples.

Beware

Inspection trips may seem a cheap way of enjoying a few days in Spain but they can turn out to be an expensive mistake. Particularly if you leave your common sense at the airport. Three out of four people who go on an inspection trip sign on the dotted line and hand over their reservation fee before their return journey home. If you are tempted to buy, go home first and think it over rather than get caught up making decisions in the heat of the moment that you may come to regret later on.

THE BUILDING PLOT

On your inspection trip you will be shown possible building plots that you can choose from. Make sure that when making your choice of plot you ask exactly how many properties you will be surrounded by. The plot you are being shown, will in all likelihood, be in an area where there are no immediate dwellings nearby and could well be in a seemingly empty field. It is important when making your decision that you visualise the area once it is built up. Urbanisation, as the Spanish like to call it, can involve the building of thousands of villas in one development alone. What could seem like an isolated spot on the inspection trip could well turn out to be in the midst of a massive housing development with villas all crammed on top of one another!

If I am shown a building plot that I like, what is the next stage?

In order to secure the plot of your choice, you will generally be asked to hand over a 2,000 euro, non-refundable reservation fee. The rest of the payments that you will have to make will be referred to as stage payments. These will vary depending on which developer you choose to buy from. An average payment scale will be a 40% deposit within thirty days, followed by the final 60% due on completion. These stage payments will, of course, vary with each development.

THE CONTRACT PRICE

The contract price should be a fixed price in euros. This will guarantee that should the currency rate alter in relation to sterling (whether the euro goes up or down), the contract price remains the same. To the contract price you will need to add an extra 7% for Spanish IVA, which is the Spanish equivalent of VAT.

ESCROW ACCOUNT

When considering purchasing off plan, make sure that your contract states that your payments will be paid into an Escrow account that the developer has no access to until the property is complete. Most of the reputable developers offer this plan. The bank then guarantees the sums you have paid if anything goes wrong.

WILL MY PROPERTY BE READY WITHIN THE AGREED TIME SCALE?

Most developers will give you a completion date of anything from nine months to two years. It would be advisable to consider this date only as a guideline as the construction process, more often than not, takes longer than anticipated, particularly if the time estimated for completion is shorter rather than longer. The developer's agent may well give you a date that is not realistic in order to get you hooked on buying the property. When I spoke to people who had actually bought in a development, they advised me that two years was the average most of them had to wait before their villa was complete. Some developers may offer compensation should the building plan go over schedule, but this is often difficult to get without an expensive legal wrangle.

WHAT CAN GO WRONG?

◆ If your deposit is not paid into an Escrow account then some developers may use the stage payment money to complete other villas which were purchased before yours.

◆ The urbanisation is illegal.

◆ Unpaid taxes.

◆ Unregistered title deeds (Escritura).

◆ Difficulty in obtaining municipal services.

◆ No planning permission.

Debts related to the property

When purchasing in Spain it is important that your Spanish legal representative checks there are no debts related to the property. In Spanish law you will be responsible for these debts.

SPANISH LAWYERS

It is advisable to use a Spanish lawyer as they will understand the 'ins and outs' of buying in Spain, perhaps more so than a British solicitor who speaks Spanish! It is important that you get sound legal advice before you commit to any purchase. Advise your lawyer that you will require the contract to be translated into your own language.

Finding a Spanish lawyer

If you want to find out where to contact a good Spanish lawyer, ask advice from people you know. If you do not know of anyone or cannot find any satisfied clients, contact the British or American Consulate who can provide you with a list of lawyers in your area who speak English, although they will not officially be allowed to recommend one.

How much are my legal expenses likely to be?

Estimate to pay about 1% of the value of the transaction. Make sure that you have agreed the costs before you instruct your lawyer. Other costs you may be responsible for include:

- opening of a Spanish bank account
- preparation of Spanish identification numbers
- financial advice (both in home country and upon arrival in Spain)
- arranging a Spanish will
- house insurance – contents and building (includes premium payment)
- connection of water and electricity (includes connection fee)
- fiscal representation
- assistance when signing the title deed.

Escritura Publica (house deed)

The 'Escritura Publica' is the registered title deed of the property. It is inscribed in the property registry. This deed is the only rock solid proof of title to land and property in Spain. If your seller, be it a developer or a private sale cannot produce their Escritura Publica then all may not be what it seems. The title deed contains details of the description and location of the property. If there are any debts, such as mortgages against the property, they will be registered in the margins of the house deeds. It is wise to see the title deeds, if only as proof that the seller actually owns the property. It is also important because it details the land the property stands on, as sometimes this important detail can be omitted! If your seller is unable to supply you with this deed and you are determined to purchase you could ask for a 'Nota Simple'.

Nota Simple

This can be obtained by your lawyer from the registry containing the relevant details and any mortgages against the property. You can also access this on the Internet if you are entered in the Registry. It is always preferable, however, to see the Escritura Publica if possible.

Purchasing a property without an Escritura Publica (house deed)

It is not uncommon for many property purchases in Spain to change hands several times without anyone actually having the Escritura

Publica. In the UK the house deeds become yours on completion, but in Spain it can take several months, if not years, to obtain the house deeds. Personally, this practice makes me nervous and I would again advise caution where the Escritura Publica is not readily available or at least available within an agreed legal timeframe. Whilst researching this chapter in Spain and talking to several Spanish property owners, I only met one British couple who actually had their Escritura Publica, the others were still waiting, for one reason or another! Some of the reasons can be:

- The developer is avoiding the payment of transfer taxes and fees which can total 10% or even more of the value.
- The owner may want to conceal assets from a creditor, taxman or spouse.
- The property has never been declared to the taxman (if previously owned).
- There is a dispute with the developer.

Case study: Joy and Ray Cox

We (or rather my husband) always had this dream of owning a retirement home in a warmer climate such as Spain. We chose Spain as we wanted a sunny destination that did not involve long flights and was reasonably close to home. We bought 'off plan' and waited for the villa to be completed. Estimated time 18 months ... real time 3 years! This wait was very stressful, more so for me, as I was not keen on the idea in the first place. It is always 'manana' for the Spanish, meaning tomorrow in our language and 'manana' can mean weeks away to Spanish builders! As a person gets older they do not want to wait indefinitely. You feel your time is running out all too quickly and you want to get on with life and enjoy it.

▶

After the long three years of waiting the villa was ready and finally ours, but not the land! We are still waiting for the legal document known as the 'Escritura'. At our age we do not need hassle and worry. All we want to do is to sit back and relax in the Spanish sunshine, if only the Spanish law would let us!

IBI receipt

This mainly concerns second hand properties. When purchasing a re-sale, you must always ask to see the paid up receipt for the IBI, before signing any contract. Otherwise you may find yourself liable for back taxes or penalties. The IBI will show the official assessed value of the property and this will be what relevant taxes will be based on. Generally the assessed value of a property will be considerably less than the market value. The IBI is the tax set by the local authority and is similar to the 'council tax' system operating in the UK. If the IBI payment is late, a 20% surcharge can be added. If you are not resident in Spain, and in order to avoid forgetting payment, you can arrange for this charge to be debited from your account.

Catastro

This is a reference number and every property must have one. It will be noted on the IBI receipt. This reference (Referencia Catastral) will contain all the details relating to the property, including boundaries, property description and location. If there are any major discrepancies between the particulars you have been given by the estate agent and the Catastro, you can assume that something may be wrong. Without the Catastro you will not officially know the true boundaries of your property and this could involve problems further down the line should you choose to sell. It is always better to be safe than sorry, no matter what the estate agent may say! If you want to see relevant documentation relating to your purchase, don't be put off even if it is inconvenient for the seller or the seller's agent.

New properties

A new property purchased from a developer will not yet have an IBI receipt. It will be your responsibility to register the property for this tax. Make sure your developer has made a declaration of a new building and has paid the small registration tax associated with this.

Community fees

These are the fees that you will be responsible for if you buy an apartment, townhouse or villa in an urbanisation area. They are similar to service charges in the UK. In a building they will include such things as:

- communal gardens
- pools
- lifts
- reception areas.

In an urbanisation they will include:

- roads
- lighting
- communal areas.

The receipt for any community fees paid will give you an indication of what your monthly charges may be. It is also advisable to see the minutes from any meetings relating to these charges as they will highlight any difficulties you may encounter when purchasing the property.

Town urban plan

If you want to make sure that no new road is planned at the bottom of your Spanish garden ask your lawyer to check the 'Plan General de Ordenacion Urbana'.

If you are purchasing in Spain from a non-resident

If you are purchasing from a non-resident in Spain you will have to pay a 5% deposit to the Hacienda (the tax office), in the seller's name, as a guarantee that he will pay his taxes. You will need a Form 211 to justify your payment and you will have to show this to the Notary (a government-appointed lawyer), as proof that you have made this payment. This payment serves as a guarantee against the non-resident seller's Spanish Capital Gains Tax liability. This 5% will be deductible from the purchase price.

Spanish bank accounts/fiscal representatives

You will need a Spanish bank account in order to pay your electricity and water charges by direct debit. A fiscal representative will make payments of your rates at the town hall on your behalf and make sure that your annual property tax is paid.

Do I have to pay for my Spanish property in euros?

You can pay for your property in euros with a cheque through a Spanish bank account. You can also pay by cheque in a foreign currency. You can also pay by direct transfer from your foreign bank to the seller's foreign bank, so that no money enters Spain.

Can I get a Spanish mortgage?

Mortgages of 20 and 30 years, plus 100% mortgages are now available in Spain. If you are a non-resident purchaser, however, the maximum you will be allowed to borrow will probably be 70% of the property's value. Spanish bank mortgages are currently amongst the lowest in Europe with rates being offered at less than 5%.

Other costs you may incur

Always have the facts about the property and exactly what is being included in the asking price carefully checked by your own legal representative. A reputable estate agent, who is offering a reputable property for sale will have no objection to you doing this. If there are objections, take that as a warning sign that all may not be as 'golden' as it is made out to be. I spoke to one British investor in Spain who told me that investing in an off plan Spanish property was like a dripping tap . . . once you had paid the initial deposit, there was a constant drip to pay more. Extras included items such as:

- white goods
- water heaters
- central heating
- terracing
- swimming pool
- paying for the Escritura.

TO SUMMARISE

Before signing anything or handing over any money, there are certain guidelines you should try to follow:

- Get advice from a Spanish lawyer.
- Ask to see the Escritura and the Nota Simple.
- Check the IBI receipt.
- Check the Catastral certificate.
- See paid up receipts for community fees.
- See paid up receipts for all utility bills.
- Get a translation of the contract into your own language.
- Make a decision about your form of payment.
- Arrange the payment of fees, taxes and the 5% deposit if buying from a non-resident.
- Get a decision regarding when you will get your final Escritura.

THE VILLA ITSELF

Surprise, surprise, villas can actually be very cold inside, even when it is warm outside. They are not built like British houses and have little insulation. If you are thinking about spending a lot of time in your property during the off-peak season consider the central heating factor. Although such a system will be expensive to install, it may well prove to be economical in the end, particularly if you later come to rely on electric heaters. Electricity in Spain is expensive. Another alternative would be to install a solar heating system.

The terrace

When you are shown your villa make sure the exterior of the landscaping of the villa is included, this will involve levelling the land, tiling around the terrace and pool area. If it is not included make sure you get an estimate as to how much this work will cost as it can be very expensive. In many urbanisations where this is not included, you could end up with endless villas sitting in sandy building mounds where DIY abounds. I visited a development recently where the majority of the villas were not sitting in pretty tiled terraced gardens, but in messy building plots and some of them had been like that for years!

Big developments

Make sure you know how big the urbanisation intends to spread. You could end up living in a glorified building site for ten years which would mean living with constant building dust and noise.

Capital gains tax

The non-resident's capital gains tax is 35% of the profit. As of December 31st 1996, Spain ended their tax exemption for property owners of over ten years and introduced an inflation correction factor. Even with this, the capital gains tax bill will still be considerable, and you will have to factor this in when calculating your profits. Another cost factor to consider will be estate agent's fees which are more sub-stantial than in the UK and range from 5% to 10%.

Income tax

Non-resident owners of Spanish property are required by law to declare 2% of the official rated value of the property as if it were income. They must pay tax on this income and as a non-resident the income tax rate is 25%.

Getting there

EasyJet and Ryan Air offer cheap flights. How long these flights will remain cheap is something to consider. You will also pay more for flights during peak holiday times. The approximate journey to Spain is two hours flying time. Do not forget to calculate into your travel time how long it will take you to travel from the airport to your Spanish des-tination. If it is a long distance from the airport this could affect the desirability of your property from a re-sale point of view, should you want to sell.

Time zone

Spain is one hour ahead of GMT and increases to two hours during the British summertime.

The golden mile

The most prestigious area on the Costa del Sol is between Marbella and Puerto Banus. One of the new up-and-coming areas is situated between Estepona and Marbella. Some experts think that the area is now becom-ing over priced and over developed, so obviously you will need to consider this if you choose to buy there.

The golf factor

Golf is emerging as a massive attraction in Spain. There are literally golf courses sprouting up all over. If your property is not situated on the coast then its proximity to a golf course will greatly increase your property's appeal for both re-sale and the rental market. For more information on golf see Chapter 12, Taking up a Sport.

Currency, tourist board and consulates

The currency is the euro and tourist information can be obtained from www.spain.info. The British Consulate can be found in Alicante, tel: 96 521 6022. The Irish Consulate is in Barcelona and can be contacted at tel: 93 491 5021.

Average daytime temperatures

◆ January/February 15°–16°
◆ March/April 18°–20°
◆ May/June 22°–24°
◆ July/August 28°–30°
◆ September/October 30°–25°
◆ November/December 15°–18°

WARNING!

Land grab is notorious in Valencia but the practice is spreading and is now affecting Andalusia. The idea behind this 'reprehensible' legislation was to regulate the acquisition and development of land. Thousands of property owners have been ensnared by this, many of them Brits, who have had their land snatched from them by developers paying well below market value and peanuts in compensation. They have also been forced to contribute financially to new infrastructures such as roads and sewers . . . all of these things were not pointed out to them at the point of sale. So buyers beware!

THE FRENCH CONNECTION

A lot of Brits dream of owning a property in France. It has breathtaking scenery, a varied cultural history and is renowned for its fine wines and excellent cuisine. It also boasts stunning architecture, a vibrant café society and many art treasures. The geography of the country is varied from the mountainous regions of the Alps and the Pyrenees, to the glamorous attractions of the South of France, particularly Nice and St Tropez, to the more gentle area of Provence. If you are lured by the attraction of fine wines then the areas of Bordeaux and Burgundy should be of particular interest.

'SPENDING THE KIDS' INHERITANCE'

If you buy a property in France and want to leave it to your family after your death, this will be governed by French law. This is a complicated tax and you will need to seek professional advice about this before committing yourself to a retirement home in France. Your legal heirs will have entrenched rights to a certain proportion of your French estate. This is known as the 'Reserve Legale', the remainder 'Quotit Disponible' is the amount that you can bequeath or gift. Other taxes to consider are 'tax-droits de succession' and gifts tax. Again, you would be advised to seek legal advice on any tax issues before making a purchase.

Cost of living

As in the UK, the cost of living in France can vary widely, depending on location, whether rural or city, or if an area is more fashionable than another. If you are planning to move to a particular area it would certainly be in your interests to make several visits before deciding to purchase anything. That way you can compare prices to those in the UK and get an appreciation of what your living and utility costs might be. You will also need to bear in mind that in France VAT is charged on food at 17%. Although the cost of living has risen in France over the last ten years, it still compares favourably to the UK and is generally thought to be 25% cheaper. You will also need to factor into your living costs how much tax you will be expected to pay and also what social security contributions you may be expected to make.

High taxes

The taxation in France is amongst some of the highest in Europe and traditionally this has put off some Brits from planning to retire there. There are three levels of tax rates in the UK whereas France has seven different rates. The top rate of tax in France is 49.8% compared to the top rate in the UK, which is currently 40%. However, unless the income of a retired couple exceeds 70,000 euros they would be financially better off in France during their retirement.

Pension arrangements

If your pension is still being drawn in the UK, you will need to declare this in France. Any EU member state has a double taxation agreement with France, which means that tax paid in one country acts as a tax credit in another. It would be wise to investigate your pension arrangements before moving to France and you should contact the relevant social security offices in France and the UK, so that the administrative process can begin.

What documents will I need to become a resident of France?

You will need a valid passport and with the expansion of the EU you will be required to apply for an EU resident permit, 'Carte de sejour', within three months of your arrival. This is for identification purposes. Contact the local police administration office, 'Prefecture de Police', and be prepared to produce certain documents:

◆ A valid passport and three passport photographs.
◆ Birth or marriage certificate.
◆ Proof that you receive a state pension.

SHOULD I RENT IN FRANCE FIRST BEFORE BUYING A PROPERTY?

As with any purchase abroad, and particularly with retirement in mind, it would be wise to spend some time exploring the area first. Not necessarily on a holiday basis, but renting somewhere for a longer stay to see if the dream really does live up to the reality. Consider whether you want to be isolated or near a village or small market town. Certainly for people choosing to retire to France, it would be a good idea to consider accessibility as a major advantage, unless of course you are planning another move before 'the less active years' set in!

Renting a French property

Renting property in France is extremely popular, regardless of whether or not you have a high income or a significant amount of savings. There is no rush to get on the property ladder, as there is in the UK, due to fear of escalating property prices. If you are looking for a place to rent, look in the local newspapers or in *Le Figaro*. If you are choosing to rent in Paris visit www.lefigaro.fr. Another useful magazine advertising property for rental is *De Particulier a Particulier*, contact them in France on tel: 0 810 21 22 23 or www.pap.fr. Alternatively you can rent through estate agents, known in France as 'Agents Immobiliers', but always check with them first their scale of charges. Generally, the fee should not amount to more than half a month's rental. The rent agreement is known as a 'bail' and the average agreement can vary. In general it is for three years, although three months' notice can be served at any time. Another way of renting is through a 'Proprietaires', a private landlord, but obviously renting privately will not afford you the protection of renting through an established agent. The property itself will be advertised as a number of rooms called 'pieces'. These rooms will not include the kitchen and bathroom.

What paperwork will I need to rent a property?

- A residency permit.
- Proof of current address (utility bill).
- Proof of ability to pay, details of state and private pensions.

Will I have to pay a deposit?

You will be required to pay a bond, which will be two to three times the rental. This bond is known as a 'cheque de caution'. This bond will be returned to you at the end of the tenancy, assuming that the property is kept in good condition. This is the equivalent to a dilapidation deposit which is payable on rental properties within the UK. In order to protect yourself from unscrupulous landlords, you are advised to take comprehensive photos of the property before the commencement of the tenancy and also employ a professional inventory clerk to list all items in the property and their condition.

Other charges

◆ 'Taxe d'habitation': this charge is levied in relation to the size of the property and is not dissimilar to the council tax that exists in the UK. There are however exemptions for the over 60's or if the property is uninhabitable for any reason.

◆ 'Charges Communes': this charge is for the general upkeep of the building and is similar to a service charge that exists in the UK. Check that the rent covers this charge before the commencement of the tenancy.

◆ Insurance: as in the UK, you would be advised to insure your own personal possessions within the rental property.

BUYING A PROPERTY IN FRANCE

The initial contract when purchasing a property in France is called a 'Sus-seing Prive', if prepared by an estate agent, and a 'Compromis de Vente' if drawn up by the Notaire. It is then signed by both parties and is legally binding. A minimum 10% deposit is payable at this stage which remains in a 'blocked' account at the Notaire's office until completion of the sale. At this stage the property is withdrawn from the market. This is similar to the exchange of contract procedure that exists in the UK. It is unlikely, once the deposit has been paid, for anyone to pull out, unless of course there is a financial problem. It is important to check before signing the 'Compromis' that you have sufficient funds to cover any costs involved when purchasing your French home.

RENOVATING A HOUSE IN FRANCE

Many people who decide to opt for the French way of life have already considered a renovation project to some degree. There are many properties – particularly the older stone houses – that are ripe for renovation. If you are thinking of a renovation project you may like to consider employing a 'maitre d'oeuvre' (jobbing architect) to look at the property and give you a quote. As mentioned before, you must do your research, as you do not want to end up renovating a house that will cost more than the house will ultimately be worth. By employing a maitre d'oeuvre you will get a good idea of renovation costs before you sign. The services of a maitre d'oeuvre will be vital if you decide to go ahead with the project as they will project manage and co-ordinate the local workforce. They will be in charge of the budget and timescale. If you decide to go it alone, you will need to be able to communicate with the local trades people (artisans). Anyone who has ever had any building work done in the UK will know how difficult it is even when you speak the language! My advice would be to employ the services of a professional . . . after all it is your retirement and who needs the hassle! The truth is, it will probably be more economical to use someone local rather than to try and 'juggle' it yourself . . . no matter how good you are at DIY!

SURVEYS

Surveys are not the same in France as they are in the UK, where three options are available: the valuation, homebuyer's report and the full structural survey (see Chapter 14, Staying Put or Moving On?). In France, it is more usual for a local builder to give an opinion on the state of the property and what areas will need to be renovated. The builder will provide quotations for the work. These can often be widely off the mark and it would be prudent to source an expert/architect's opinion on aspects of the property you are considering refurbishing, if only to get an idea of the costs involved from an independent party. It is unlikely, however, that they would provide a full written report, as this practice is not necessarily followed in some European countries. However, it is most important before signing the binding 'Compromis', particularly in rural locations, that you know exactly what costs are involved, be it from the installation of a septic tank to a new roof.

Who can I approach to carry out the valuation report?

Notaires will often be able to provide assistance. Some offices have qualified staff that are able to carry out a valuation. Notaires can work for both parties. They work for the government as official tax collectors and solicitors. These valuations, however, can be based more on the legal side than the practical side. Another solution regarding the survey would be to contact an Expert Immobilier/Agent Immobilier. It is their job to provide information relevant to the purchaser's needs with regard to the condition and value of the property. These experts cover most aspects of private housing and can easily be found by contacting the: Chambre des Experts Immobiliers de France FNAIM or visit www.experts-fnaim.org.

What information can I expect in the report?

◆ Confirmation that the vendor does own the property for sale.
◆ To check out the land being purchased in the 'Releve Cadastral' and to make sure that all the land being sold is accurately documented.
◆ To check the 'Cadastral' plan on the ground, since a greater or lesser amount of land can affect the valuation.

Consultation of the 'Plan d'Occupation des Sols'

This, in essence, is the planning notation in which the property is located. For instance, if the building is located within a NC zone, only certain renovation/refurbishments will be allowed. This could affect the overall value of the property; for example, if restrictions were in place which prevented any extensions. These restrictions will also be apparent when the notary obtains a 'Certificat d'Urbanisme' (the main planning document) but this will be much later down the line.

- The consideration of any 'rights of way' over the property.
- To clarify services offered such as water, electricity or sewerage.
- To ascertain whether refurbishment costs will end up costing more than the overall value of the property. This means determining with the buyer what essential works need to be undertaken and also to establish what future additional improvements the buyer may want to make.
- To estimate the value of the property once those improvements have been carried out. If no improvements are necessary, then to value the property in its current condition. This may be determined by comparing other properties recently sold within a localised area.
- New build properties will be valued by the 'Expert Immobilier' using methods such as calculating the value of the land and adding to this any construction costs.

Caution

The 'Expert Immobilier' will usually work within one area and will be well equipped with knowledge about local land values and building costs. Non-French purchasers without proper advice could find themselves being charged an inflated price for their property. They will not necessarily be familiar with the local economy and land values. This could prove problematic when the property is put up for sale, as the property may be too expensive for the local market and, therefore, will limit the re-sale potential to overseas investors only.

Completion

This is the completion date (as we know it) which the Notaire will have set. This can sometimes be set well in advance, but can be brought forward once all the paperwork and searches have been completed. This is the point of sale when the property becomes yours in total and you are given the house deeds 'Acte Authentiques'. The Notaire's fees will also have to be paid on completion and they can vary from 8%–10% for the purchase of a property more than five years old, and 3%–4% for the purchase of new properties.

ADDITIONAL FEES

If you are taking out a French mortgage there will be a fixed charge of 1 to 2% of the mortgage payable to the Notaire. There will also be a mortgage arrangement fee. Other fees can be subject to VAT depending on what type of property you are buying, how much land it has and whether you intend to cultivate the land or not.

Taxation

Tax 'Fonciere' is a tax paid by the owner of a French property. This is a land tax that is generally paid in a one off sum on the January 1st each year. It can sometimes be divided between the purchaser and the seller. If it is to be divided, this should be written into the contract of sale.

Home insurance

The most common insurance plan in France is the 'Multirisques Habitation'. This covers not only the structure of the building, but also the contents. As with any insurance policy it is always sensible to check the small print, as it may be obvious what it does cover, but it may not be so clear on what it doesn't. In essence the more comprehensive your insurance policy, the more you will pay.

Health insurance

The French health system requires a certain amount of personal contribution, so most residents have some kind of insurance to help cover the costs. The most the state will pay is around 70% of the total cost, so it will be necessary for most residents to top this up with an insurance policy. There is a choice of insurance policies available which range from a full private health plan or a 'top up' insurance known as 'complementaire' or 'mutuelle'.

Car insurance

Some car insurance companies in France offer breakdown cover such as 'Europ Assistance', see www.europ-assistance.com. Check whether any policy you are considering taking out offers this cover.

Driving in France

British nationals who live in France for over a year no longer need to exchange their UK licence for a French one. If, however, you prefer to have a French driving licence then you will need to return your UK licence back to the DVLA on receipt of getting your French one. To obtain a French driving licence you will need to apply to the local 'Prefecture'. If you take your own car to France, you will need to change the registration number to a French numberplate. Further information relating to driving in France can be obtained from: Ministere des Transports, tel: 00 33 14081 82 48/82 12 or 81 87 or visit www.cemt.org.

What is a prefecture?

The prefecture is an administration that belongs to the Interior Ministry and is in charge of issuing identity cards, driving licences, passports, residence and work permits for foreigners, car registration, registration of associations and the management of police and fire fighters. There are around a hundred prefectures in France.

Opening a French bank account

As a resident in France, you will need to open a bank account. If you have a limited command of the French language, you may find that a bank used to dealing with expatriates is your best option. You will need to check with each bank what facilities they offer and how often interest payments are made on savings accounts. It is worth noting that no interest is paid on current accounts. Other considerations to bear in mind when shopping around for the best account are:

◆ Do they offer on-line/telephone banking?
◆ Are there restrictions regarding the number of withdrawals?
◆ What are the charges for transfers to euro/non-euro accounts?

You will also need to provide proof of identification when opening an account and proof of residency status.

TAKING YOUR PETS WITH YOU

There are certain requirements that will have to be met when planning to take your cat, dog or both to their new home.

◆ They will need to have an EU passport. The passport will have information about the name and address of the owner and vaccination information. Only veterinary inspectors can issue these. Check with your practice to see if they issue passports.
◆ All cats and dogs must be microchipped for identification purposes.
◆ From 2004 all cats and dogs are required to have a blood test to prove they have had the rabies vaccination. The vaccine must take place at least 30 days before the blood test.

USEFUL FORMS TO OBTAIN

E106: this form provides medical cover for up to two years and is particularly relevant to those receiving a private pension and, as yet, not a state one. Contact your local Department of Social Services (DSS) for further information. When the E106 form expires, and you still do not qualify for a state pension, you may need to consider taking out private insurance or making voluntary contributions. It is worth speaking to your local French social security office regarding this.

E121GB: this form applies to people who only receive a state pension or, at a later date, an EU pension. This will allow them to register for health care in France. This form is available from the DSS.

SA29: this leaflet explains your social security and health care rights in the European community. More information about any of these issues can be obtained from tel: 0191 213 5000.

Climate
France is a large country with four climate regions.

- Inland: the climate is continental with cold winters, hot summers and medium rainfall.
- Oceanic-covering mid-west France and the northwest: this region has cool summers, frequent rain and mild winters.
- Mountainous regions: the Alps and Pyrenees. This region has very cold, snowy winters and hot, dry summers.
- Mediterranean: from the coast to 50km inland. The Mediterranean has mild winters, sometimes heavy rain and hot, dry summers.

For more information on the French climate visit www.meteo.fr.

THE FRENCH WAY OF LIFE AND ITS REGIONS
The French way of life requires shopping several times a week at small markets or well-stocked supermarkets that carry quality produce. It involves cooking with herbs and fresh foods, not processed ones. You

can swim in the warm waters of the Cote d'Azur . . . ski down the beautiful mountains and glaciers in the Alps . . . visit the chateaux and enjoy the wines of the Loire valley, see the dramatic coast line of Brittany and the golden sands of the Atlantic . . . it is your choice. As there is something for everyone . . . the hardest decision is where to go!

Burgundy

Burgundy is famous for its wines and countryside. The capital Dijon is a cultural city with museums, restaurants, music. The city is still relatively cheap, if you avoid the Parisian second home hotspots. Prices went up by 7% last year, but it is still regarded as one of the cheapest areas of France. The nearest airports are Paris and Lyons. Winters are cold, but it is very popular with retirees.

Brittany and Normandy

The British have been emigrating to Brittany since Norman times, but that still doesn't make them any more popular. It is mainly locals resenting house price rises, although it has to be conceded that Brits tend to buy up old ruins and revitalise decaying villages. House prices are reasonable in Brittany and Normandy. Brittany has more than one thousand miles of coastline and many medieval towns and castles. Rennes, the capital of Brittany, is only two hours by train from Paris. There are plenty of areas along the coastline that offer wonderful retirement opportunities for the 'young at heart' amongst a young population. Rennes has two universities and hosts up to 60,000 students.

The Dordogne and Bordeaux

Bordeaux is a rich and beautiful city that has been financed over the years through its booming wine trade. The centre has been regenerated with a new tramway and it represents an easily accessible city for those who prefer a more urban style retirement. The Dordogne is very popular with Brits packing their bags for foreign shores and some areas have become very British with cricket teams and Marmite being offered! House prices have slowed in the area with vendors having to reduce their prices. If you are looking for a more rural retirement then this could be the area for you – if you are not concerned about being isolated.

The Alps

This area offers some of the best skiing in the world. It is a must for winter sports enthusiasts. Val d'Isere and Tignes are for the more serious skier whilst families are welcomed at Meribel. If you are looking for somewhere to retire to and ski your socks off, then look at where the developers are moving in and where they are buying land. It is much cheaper than in the south.

Languedoc-Roussillon

Here the climate is Mediterranean. It's the world's biggest vineyard. The region is considered to be a very healthy place to live which is great if you are looking for somewhere to retire to. It boasts little industry, so no significant air pollution, and offers fish, olive oil and fresh fruit as its home grown produce. It's easy to reach on the high speed train from Paris and the lifestyle is laid back. Montpelier is the capital and the whole area would suit wine lovers and sun worshippers. House prices have increased over the last few years, but have stablised with cheaper housing further away from the coast.

Pays de la Loire

Nantes, the capital, is consistently voted the best place to live in France by the French media. It is close to the sea with a lively cultural centre including theatres, restaurants and bars nestling on cobbled streets. 'The Vendee' has a hundred miles of sandy beaches and property prices are more expensive on the coast than they are inland. The Pays de la Loire has been declared a world heritage site by Unesco which calls it a 'cultural landscape of exceptional beauty'. The climate is warmer than the

UK and if you want somewhere different to retire to then this area might be what you are looking for.

Provence

Famous, not just because of the book *A Year in Provence*, but also because of its fantastic climate and stunning scenery. It has both mountains and the sea and is very popular with Brits. If you are thinking of retiring to Provence to get away from the British then you could be disappointed, as this place is full of them. Properties on the Riviera are expensive and overpriced. Any properties on the coast will go at a premium . . . so that little retirement home in St Tropez may well be out of reach for the average retiree. Cheaper properties can be found in Luberon, a mountainous region in western Provence. The region's capital is Marseilles, France's oldest city, which is currently trying to live down its reputation as being the drug capital of France. Aix-en-Provence may be more suitable for those wanting to retire and have an urban lifestyle. Nice and Cannes might suit the rich 'shopaholic' and beach bum . . . perfect for the retiree who is determined to 'Spend The Kids' Inheritance'!

CAN I MAKE MONEY OUT OF MY FRENCH PROPERTY TO HELP WITH MY RETIREMENT?

Being a permanent resident in France, you can generate a good income by running self-catering accommodation complexes. These do not necessarily have to be on a large scale and it could even be a B&B. The season can run from June until September, with other popular breaks being Easter, Christmas and the UK spring bank holiday. There are potentially 20 weeks of the year for generating good rental income. If you are planning to run a 'gite' in your retirement, you will want to consider where the good tourist areas are. You may also want to consider whether a renovation project is for you, as doing up a large farmhouse, for example, with out-buildings could provide an excellent base for starting off your self-catering business. A chateau could also be something you may consider particularly if you are looking at a B&B option, but you will need to bear in mind that there is not a great 're-sale' market for a chateau.

THE ITALIAN JOB

Italy is brimming with cultural history spanning many centuries. It is the birthplace of many of the world's greatest artists and home to many of the finest art treasures. If you are considering retiring to Italy a trial period of renting before you make your purchase will help you decide if an area suits you – especially in winter! It is also important to consider how remote you want to be, as what might seem like an idyllic retreat in your 60s, might seem too isolated in your 70s, so if you are not considering moving again, you will want to be close to amenities and have access to good health facilities.

Retiring to Italy can be a very attractive proposition as Italy enjoys long, hot, dry summers. The nearer to the coast you are, the cooler the summers are likely to be although it is worth remembering that in some areas the winters can be cold. You will need to research the temperatures in the region of your choice.

Applying for residency

All EU citizens planning to retire to Italy will need to apply for a resident's permit (Permesso di Soggiorno) and this should be done within eight days of arrival. You will be required to register with the local police authority, the 'Questura', and complete paperwork to obtain the permit necessary to legalise your stay. The permit is specifically for the area where you live. You then need to register with the Statistics Bureau, or 'Anagrafe'. For the permit you will need to take with you:

- Photocopies of the first page in your passport (and visa, if you have one).
- Three passport photos.
- Proof of health insurance.
- Proof of financial security such as pensions (both state and private).
- After you have settled into your new home you can then exchange your permit for a full residence certificate (Certificato di Residenza).

Italian estate agents

Finding a home in a foreign country can be a very difficult and expensive process. The Internet is a great research tool and can give you an initial idea of what you are looking for. Most of the sites are in Italian, but the pictures and prices will give you a good idea of what you should be paying for a property, which location you can afford to live in and what kind of property you would prefer to purchase. Once you have that information you will be ready to embark on a thorough search of your chosen area. When you have decided upon the place you would like to retire to, it may be a good idea to consider dealing directly with Italian estate agents. They spend a lot of their time focusing on Italian buyers, and usually have access to a far larger selection of properties in more locations and price ranges than what may be found in traditional tourist areas where foreigners could be exploited.

Once you have found the place you want to buy

There will be a procedure in place which you must follow in order to purchase your property.

- You will need to agree a price and sign a 'compromesso di vendita' (preliminary contract).
- You will pay a deposit (usually between 10%–30%).
- Upon completion both parties sign a document called 'il rogito notarile' and the balance and fees are paid as appropriate.

- Total fees for buying property vary but are usually between 10%–15%. If you are looking for a mortgage from an Italian lender, the typical deposit amount would be around 20%.
- A purchase registration tax of 3–4% is payable if the property is the principal place of residence. If the property is not a principal place of residence then a tax of 10% is payable. Finally, a local property tax called ICI (Imposta Comunale Surgli Immobili) of 0.4–0.7% of the property value is also payable.
- Also, be aware that buyers inherit unpaid debts on a property and property can be repossessed and sold by a lender or local authority to pay a debt.

Surveyor/architect/geometra

You may need to employ the services of a 'geometra'. They are the combination of a surveyor and an architect and are employed to make sure that the correct documentation is prepared for sale. It is worth shopping around for a good 'geometra' especially if you plan to do any renovation work. Some people say a good geometra can make all the difference to a smooth running building programme, although others (see Villa Sibillini at the end of this chapter) would have preferred to use an architect from the start. Ask around the local area for recommendations and visit properties the geometra has worked on previously. Try and talk to the owners to see if they were happy with the work.

Italian mortgages

A mortgage (un mutuo) is money lent by a financial institution secured against the borrower's property. The same rules apply essentially as in the UK. If the borrower is unable to meet the payments stipulated in the mortgage contract their property can be repossessed by the lender. Italian mortgages usually last 5, 10, 15 or 20 years, although they can last sometimes as long as 25 or 30 years. Usually the mortgage will cover 80% of the value of the property, although some banks offer finance up to 100% of that value (sometimes requesting extra guarantees and with stricter conditions). It is also important to note that in Italy all mortgages have to be paid off by the age of 70. So, if you are considering retiring to Italy, visit www.mutuionline.com for more detailed information on what mortgages are on offer and how to request a mortgage.

Home insurance

The consensus seems to be that insurance in Italy is much cheaper than the UK. House insurance is normally a condition of your mortgage agreement, but do check this if you are buying a property.

Buying off plan

New property laws in Italy will mean that any builder selling any 'off plan' property will have to obtain a bank guarantee for the amount of money he expects to take from the purchaser. This will cover the buyer should the builder go bust. The developer has to provide a guarantee (fideiussione) before the contract is signed and any money is handed over. The guarantee can be granted by a bank or an insurance company, for example. The developer also has to take out a ten year insurance policy (similar to the NHBC/Zurich policy which we have in the UK). This covers any defects that might occur in the property. The new law also states that all issues relating to the build, including planning permission, builder's details and schedule of works must be listed in the sale contract.

Properties to look out for

If you are retiring to Italy you might be looking for a renovation project. If this is the case, you can pick up a cheaper property in Italy if you are prepared to put up with all of the hard work associated with doing up a ruin. Obviously, this will be a challenge and an even harder one if you don't speak the language. Other cheaper properties can be found in rural locations generally with land attached. There are also 'half reno-vated' properties to be found where all the structural work is done and you are just left with the creative bit. I certainly think that buying some-thing with all the structural work done is an advantage anywhere, but especially in a foreign country. That is if you can afford the premium.

Life insurance

This is likely to be a condition of your mortgage, but do check to be on the safe side.

Medical insurance/health care

As a resident of Italy, you will need various kinds of insurance. The first of these is health insurance which is compulsory for all foreign residents in Italy. Proof of health cover must be shown to the local authorities before you can obtain a residence permit.

The local health authority (L'unita sanitaria locale)

After you have obtained your residence permit, you will be required to register with your local health authority (L'unita sanitaria locale) to obtain your national health number. You will then be able to register with a doctor, known in Italy as 'medico convenzionato'. Retired people from EU countries should bring their Form E121. Also, if you take reg-ular medication in your home country, find out its generic name from your doctor (not its brand name) to avoid any confusion.

The Italian national health system (Servizio Sanitario Nazionale)

This system offers low-cost health care of a good standard, but the downside is that the waiting lists can be long. Private health insurance is very popular because of this and the 'no frills' amenities of the state hospitals. Emergency treatment is available to everyone. EU citizens benefit from reciprocal health agreements and will need to bring their Form E111 or the new European Health Insurance Card (EHIC).

Your pension situation

Investigate your pension situation and inform the benefits agency in your home country before you leave. UK citizens can call the International Pensions Centre on tel: 0191 218 7777 or visit www.guide-information.org.uk.

Bank accounts

Most banks will only allow foreigners to open an account if they possess the full residence certificate (certificato di residenza), as opposed to the 'permesso di soggiorno'. It is better to open an account with a bank that has branches near you so that any problems that may occur can be solved directly. If you do not have a certificato di residenza, you could approach Italian banks that have offices in the UK. The bank's office in the UK can then liaise with your chosen branch in Italy. You will need to bring certain documents with you to open an account:

◆ A valid passport.
◆ A valid certificato di residenza.
◆ Proof of your address in Italy, such as a utility bill, telephone bill or rental contract.
◆ Your birth certificate.
◆ Pension details or a reference from your home bank.

Driving in Italy

To own a car in Italy you need a full 'certificato di residenza'. To register or buy a car you also need a tax code number known as 'codice fiscale'. Non-residents with a 'permesso di soggiorno' can drive on a foreign or international licence until they have lived in Italy for a year. The International Licence is preferable – apply in your home country before you leave. The following points apply to driving in Italy:

- The EU licence has to be authenticated at the nearest 'Motorizzazione'.
- To exchange a foreign licence for an Italian one can be complicated. 'Pratiche Automobilistiche Agenzie' can help you with your application.
- Italy has reciprocal agreements with certain countries regarding licences.

REGIONS

From the sunny southern slopes of the Alps to the lush orange groves of Sicilia, Italy has plenty to offer with stunning scenery and diverse historical backgrounds. This is in part due to the fact that Italy grew up as a collection of independent city-states. As a result of which customs and food varies greatly from region to region. Travellers in ancient times gave the country its first name as 'Land of Wines', and this probably accounts for the fact that the Italians are considered natural hosts. As a result of this, Italy is one of the most popular vacation countries in Europe. Throughout most of the year the beaches are sunny and you can usually find waters where the temperature is right for swimming. In summer, Italy is an international playground with visitors from all continents mingling with vacationing Italians at the famous resorts. Spring comes early to Italy and autumn lingers. Large cities and holiday resorts such as those in the Lombardian Lake Region are particularly splendid at these times of year. In winter, the Italian Alps are unparalleled for scenery and skiing. In northern Italy there are some of the world's most renowned winter sports resorts.

Le Marche

Is still largely an agricultural area which is essentially mountainous and hilly. Le Marche is located on the eastern side of Italy between the Apenine Mountains and the Adriatic Sea. The mountain area is rugged with deep gorges and rushing streams. Marche remains untouched by massive tourism and has a rich mix of history, architecture, beautiful countryside and sandy beaches. If you are a food lover, Le Marche could be the area for you. From spring through to autumn, every town and village will celebrate its speciality. Le Marche is particularly famous for its pecorino sheeps milk and its truffles, but every kind of food is celebrated from polenta to wild boar. The regional capital is Ancona. Other important cities are Ascoli, Piceno, Urbino, Macerate and Pesaro. The coastline presents a succession of gently rolling hills and flat plains crossed by rivers.

Tuscany

Tuscany is world famous. It has enchanted landscapes, coastline, museums, cathedrals, buildings of historical interest and towns like Florence, Pisa, and Siena. Tuscany is full of Etruscan and ancient Roman ruins. Medieval Tuscany is still visible in the small walled towns. Some of the ruins are well preserved, but are generally not to be found on the tourist route.

Tuscany's landscape

The region stretches over the slope of the Apenines, in front of the Tyrrehenian Sea and is mountainous and hilly. Cities such as Florence, the capital of Tuscany, and Siena, Pisa, Arezzo, Pistoia, Lucca, Livorno, Grosseto and Massa Carrara are all located within the region. The coastline is a mixture of long sandy beaches and headlands. Just off the coast are the Archipelago islands.

Property in Tuscany

There are other attractions to Tuscany. It offers areas of outstanding beauty, such as the National Park of the Argentario and the Isola of Elba; all of which adds to the attraction of the region. Because of its popularity, it is difficult to find reasonably priced properties in the Tuscany area, especially in Florence/Siena and the Chianti areas where properties have always been very expensive. If you are thinking of retiring to the region then you will need to take your time getting to know the area. It is still possible to find cheap properties, but when they do come up check their surrounding location carefully as some of the cheaper properties often have the drawback of being near industrial estates.

Umbria

Umbria is not as expensive as areas like Tuscany and it is growing in attraction with the introduction of cheap flights from the UK to Perugia. The region is mostly hilly and mountainous and there are woods and lakes. Umbria is crossed by the Apennines which forms numerous valleys. Perugia is the regional capital and other important cities are Assisi, Orvieto, Gubbio, Todi, Terni and Spoleto.

LETTING OUT PROPERTY IN ITALY

The continental lifestyle is a lure for most people considering retiring abroad. If this is your plan and you are hoping to rent the property out before you retire in order to help with the financing, then you had better do your homework and consider all of the costs involved. Renting out a property is not easy money and it is very competitive with rents having stabilised over the last three years. The rental season can realistically only be guaranteed for the peak season; July and August. A pool is essential, plus having substantial bedrooms and ample bathrooms will help to rent out your property. Not having a pool will be a big drawback for holiday makers looking to rent. There will be costs involved running any property and they will only be offset by the rental income earned. It is unlikely to cover all costs: insurance, pool maintenance, gardening, cleaning and laundry services amongst other expenses. Insurance in the regions of Tuscany and Umbria can be expensive because of the threat of earthquakes. So all in all, do not expect to make money from your retirement home because, as with most holiday properties, they seldom 'wash their own face' but there are tax advantages.

Case Study: Villa Sibillini, Pam and David Bates

Pam and David Bates decided to sell up in the UK and run a B&B in Italy. They had decided they would make a new life for themselves in Italy as they had fallen in love with Le Marche after visiting relatives who worked there. Pam used to run a model agency and an event company whilst David was a bursar. They had four children and very busy working lives and hardly saw each other. When I met Pam she told me that she began thinking that there had to be more to life. Pam and David decided that they would buy a holiday home in Italy so that they could do holiday lets until the time came when they could retire there. However, that was all to change when they saw the house, Villa Sibillini, which needed a lot of work. They made an offer which was accepted. They signed the 'Compresso', paid the deposit and completed in January 2001. The house needed a lot of work doing to it and they began the programme of restoration.

Prior to this, they had made a business plan as they had decided to run a B&B and were applying for a licence. Villa Sibillini was large and fell into the 'Country House' bracket, therefore the licence they applied for also enabled them to be able to open a restaurant as well if they so wished. Pam offers sound advice to anyone thinking of opening a B&B:

> Do not try to run before you can walk. A lot of people make the mistake of trying to cater to too many people when they first open and take too many bookings. This can get them a bad reputation if the service offered is not up to scratch. It is better to take fewer bookings in the early stages until the business settles in.

Whilst restoring the villa, David was able to make himself understood in Italian to the builders. Their daughter, Georgina, speaks Italian fluently, so she was able to communicate on legal matters, which was a great relief to Pam who is in the process of learning the language.

The renovations were a big project and Pam's only regret is that she did not employ an architect instead of a geomatra. She believes an architect would have had a better vision and more control over the building project.

When I asked Pam what were the positive sides of running a B&B she replied that for her it had to be the opportunity of living in Italy. She also added that she enjoys meeting people and is happy to offer advice to anyone who may want to do the same and open a B&B. The business is very much a family affair as they all help with the cooking. Pam spent two years at catering college with Gordon Ramsey and Pam's mother also contributes to the cooking team, making delicious jams from home grown cherries, plums and figs.

The downside of running a B&B is that you are unlikely to make enough money in the first two years to cover all costs. Pam spends two hours a day marketing the business and also has to continue working some of the time in the UK for her events company. Their business plan has been carefully worked out and they estimate that, with the rennovation costs taken into consideration, they should break even this year. As prices have risen in the region, 'Villa Sibillini' is making good capital growth.

A typical day for Pam and David at Villa Sibillini would consist of the following:

- *sweeping the terrace*
- *cleaning the pool*
- *preparing breakfast and clearing away*
- *cleaning rooms and laundry*
- *any villa maintenance*
- *shopping for food*
- *serving drinks (they have a fully licensed bar)*
- *cooking dinner in the restaurant*
- *chatting to guests*

- *marketing*
- *dealing with e-mails.*

Pam has no regrets about the move, selling up their home of 17 years and starting a new life in another country because 'now I "work to live" and not "live to work" as I did in England'. 'I love running Villa Sibillini and totally embrace the Italian way of life' says Pam.

Pam can be contacted at: Villa Sibillini, Contrada Collato 10, San Ginesio 62026, Macerata, Italia. Or visit www.villasibillini.com, tel/fax: +39 0733 653 081.

Case study: Il Nascondiglio di Bacco, Silvia and Jacques

I also spoke to Silvia who runs a B&B at 'Il Nascondiglio di Bacco' (Bacchus Hide-Out) with her husband Jacques. The house was built over 500 years ago. In 2003 Silvia and Jacque sympathetically restored it. Where possible, old brick walls have been exposed and there are beamed, vaulted ceilings. The house sits on top of a small hill; the perfect location to take in a breathtaking and uninterrupted view of the surrounding area of Le Marche. Silvia says 'the scenery is spectacular' in all seasons and all weathers. Silvia explains how they decided to change their lives and open a B&B in Italy.

> *After 25 years of working in multinationals, my husband Jacques tired of his job. His passion had always been wine, and owning a vineyard was his dream. My heart had always been in Italy, coming from my Italian great-grandmother who made ravioli and the greatest pesto ever! The idea of the B&B came after realising that we would not be able to make a living on wine alone (to make a small fortune with wine, you start with a big one!).*
>
> *We chose the Le Marche region because throughout the years, Jacques and I had visited other wine regions like Rioja, Ribera del Duero, Napa Valley, Monterrey, Bordeaux and others. We found that*

prices were exorbitant and they all lacked something: a little character, charm, some magic.

A work colleague and future partner of my husband's, pointed out Le Marche as an unknown and undiscovered area with a history of good wine making. So, we fell in love with 'Offida', in the 'Ascoli Piceno' Province.

The first house we saw was 'the one', although we only knew it after scouting three thousand kilometers of 'Il Piceno'. It took a few sleepless nights, a lot of financial brainstorming to realise that selling our existing home, using some of our savings and getting a mortgage could make this adventure possible.

Speaking almost no Italian and with a phrase book in hand, we set out to hire the Geometra and the building team to work on the house. We had no clue where to begin but Jacques' previous experience developing businesses around the world from Brazil to Ukraine (among others), provided him with an instinct to detect the efficient from the charlatan. Our builder made a deal with Jacques. He would pay the electricity and Jacques would provide the wine. We soon realised we made the worst deal ever . . . as a couple of them began drinking wine as early as 8:30 am, and Jacques who had vouched to help and be part of the team, could not let them down! The build went very well and our team of men were true artisans and we enjoyed watching them work: brick by brick, tile by tile, tearing down or putting up walls, carefully but efficiently and fast.

We opened the B&B a little over a year ago. My strength to run this business is my love for people. I enjoy meeting people from all over the world and seeing people have a good time, see them relax slowly, drink wine, taste our great olive oil and eat delicious but simple food. Running a B&B does require dedication but it is very satisfying work and I am enjoying it immensely.

▶

Jacques has been doing some consulting work to help with the finances. The current 'world' situation, the currency fluctuation with countries like the USA, amongst others, has not helped our business. But soon we hope to be breaking even and eventually turning a profit, in return for a fabulous way of life with great capital gains potential.

For more information, please contact Silvia Cuneo/Jacques Bellemare at: Nascondiglio di Bacco, Contrada Ciafone, 79 63035 Offida, (AP) - Italia. Tel/fax: +39 0736 889537 or visit www.vinoffida.com.

SUMMARY

Almost a million Britons already draw their state pension abroad. It is expected that by 2010, one in eight Britons aged over 55 will be living overseas. If the trend continues, by 2020 one in five Britons over the age of 55 could be packing their suitcases for good, in search of a new life overseas. The cost of living in most retirement destinations can be considerably cheaper than in the UK, and as pension payments are less than anticipated, this could well be a lure for retirees to try pastures new and seemingly get more for their money. However, it is important before making your purchase that you discover all you can about the tax, health and insurance issues. You may want to 'Spend The Kids' Inheritance', or alternatively you may want to leave your overseas home to your kids or grandchildren, so it is important you know where you stand with regard to inheritance tax when resident abroad.

6

Health, Fitness and Looking Good

Without good health, it is very difficult to get the most out of retirement or, indeed, out of life. Some people are blessed with good health, no matter what they do whereas others have to work at it. I think it is fair to say that 'the over 50s' have to work at it a little harder. It's not necessarily a question of having rippling muscles, cellulite free thighs and flat stomachs (although it would be nice). It is more about maintaining what you have got and not letting yourself slide by becoming overweight, overindulged and downright lazy. Keeping trim and keeping your heart healthy is a harder job than it was in your 20s, but if you want to make the most of life then keeping on top of health and fitness issues is vital. Good health is one of the few things that money can't buy!

THE BASICS

This chapter will only cover the basics of a healthy diet and fitness, as there are many specialised books available which deal solely with these issues. But there is no time like the present to get started on 'looking good and feeling great'!

Is it safe for me to exercise?

It is regarded as safe for pensioners to exercise in moderation. Even patients with chronic illnesses like heart disease, high blood pressure, diabetes, and arthritis, can exercise safely. Many of these conditions are improved with exercise. If you are not sure if exercise is safe for you or if you are currently inactive, ask your doctor.

Physical activity

Just cleaning the house is a physical activity! The most important thing to remember is that any activity is better than no activity. So, if it is a question of using the stairs instead of the lift and you are capable . . . then do it. Similarly, get off the bus a stop early and walk the rest of the way home. Move around whilst on the phone, do some vigorous gardening, park the car further away from the shops so you have to walk. The motto here is 'if you don't want to lose it then you will have to use it'. The most important thing about starting any exercise programme is to set yourself realistic targets and not be too ambitious. Trying to run before you can walk will leave you discouraged and more likely to give up.

How much is too much?

Starting slowly makes it less likely that you will injure yourself. The saying 'no pain, no gain' is not true for older or elderly adults. You do not have to exercise at a high intensity to get the most health benefits.

As a rule, most adults need to do at least 30 minutes of 'moderate intensity' exercise every day at least five days a week. This can be broken down into three ten minute chunks if it fits into the day easier. The most important thing is to build up slowly and as your heart and lungs grow stronger your circulation will improve. You will begin not only to feel better, but also to look better.

Walking

Physical activity such as walking can cut your risk of a hip fracture by up to 40%, as it helps to improve your balance and strength. It can also reduce your risk of cancer, particularly colon and breast cancer. If you are going to take up walking as your form of exercise, gradually increase the speed of your walk until a brisk walk is comfortable. This is also a form of cardio-vascular exercise which helps keep the heart healthy. During exercise, you should breathe harder and feel warmer, but be able to keep active and still talk at the same time. If you think that you are unlikely to keep to a discipline of walking every day then consider buying a dog (or at least borrowing one). I have and there is no way he will let me off the hook . . . no matter what the weather! Another thing I enjoy about walking the dog is that you can really see the seasons change. It is also a very sociable activity as you inevitably get to meet other dog walkers.

Stamina, strength and flexibility

As with any exercise programme, you should choose something you enjoy and you should warm-up for five minutes before each exercise session. Walking slowly and stretching are good warm-up activities. You should also cool down with five minutes stretching when you finish exercising. Some ways to build up your stamina are:

◆ Walking, tennis, cycling, swimming, dancing and some forms of housework e.g. window cleaning.

To build up strength:

◆ Walking uphill, carrying shopping, climbing stairs, gardening, such as digging or mowing the lawn.

To build up flexibility:

◆ Yoga, pilates, dancing, t'ai chi, gardening, housework (involving bending and stretching).

When should I not exercise?

Exercise is only good for you if you are feeling well. If you have a cold, flu or other illness, wait to exercise until you feel better. If you miss exercise for more than two weeks, be sure to start slowly again. If your muscles or joints are tender the day after exercising, you may have done too much. Next time, exercise at a lower intensity. If the pain or discomfort persists, you should talk to your doctor. You should also talk to your doctor if you have any of the following symptoms whilst exercising:

◆ chest pain or pressure
◆ trouble breathing or excessive shortness of breath
◆ light-headedness or dizziness
◆ difficulty with balance
◆ nausea.

Yoga

This is one of the milder forms of exercise such as jogging and brisk walking. Yoga is particularly suitable for the elderly. The body structure changes as a person gets older and becomes less supple. Healing takes much longer and medical conditions can arise such as heart failure, high blood pressure, high cholesterol, poor circulation, mature onset diabetes and breathing difficulties. Muscular strength declines and weight may increase, making getting around more difficult and exhausting. Therefore, it is important to try and stay fit during this time.

Because the body is no longer at its peak, it will be necessary to set some limits as to the types of exercises that are suitable. Yoga is a form of exercise that adapts to your needs and abilities as it deals with your whole being. With yoga, you can learn deep breathing and relaxation techniques that will help you remain healthy, active and increase your energy levels. Incorporating the breathing techniques practised in yoga can make you feel refreshed and it can help to cleanse the air passages which assist in preventing respiratory problems. Yoga makes your body fitter, the mind calmer and more relaxed. Yoga is also beneficial in the prevention and control of common health and emotional problems that are linked with old age. It helps you become more in touch with yourself and your body, enabling you to accept who and what you are, which in turn encourages a positive approach to life.

Getting started

Know your body and respect its limits and do not try and push yourself too hard. The harder you try, the more you expose yourself to injury. If you can't do a pose then don't worry as stress and yoga don't go together. The aim of yoga is to quieten the mind, as you exercise the body and yoga can only be effective if you practise it properly. Also, if you feel pain, stop what you are doing. Remember you do not have to do all the poses and can rest when you feel tired. There are no prizes for injuring yourself! For information on yoga visit www.yoga-expert.com, or www.yogamag.net or www.discoveryhealth.co.uk.

Yoga for the disabled

You do not have to be physically mobile to practise yoga. You can do it from a bed or a chair and there are techniques developed for those who have limited mobility. For further information on yoga for those with disabilities visit www.yogainchairs.com, www.yogajp.com or www.taobooks.com.

The history of pilates

Joseph Pilates was born in 1880 near Düsseldorf, Germany. Very little is known about his early life, but he appears to have been a frail child, suffering from asthma, rickets and rheumatic fever. His drive and determination to overcome these ailments led him to become a competent gymnast, diver and skier. Joseph Pilates was interned in England during World War One and it was here that he began investigating ways he could rehabilitate himself, whilst being bed ridden. Pilates believed that mental health and physical well being had to go hand in hand and that one would not work without the other. Pilates created a method of total body conditioning based on alignment, concentration, control, being centred, precision, breathing and flowing. This resulted in increased flexibility, muscle tone, strength and mental agility. Pilates practitioners use their own bodies as 'weights' in training and this method of exercise is not focused on high-powered cardio-vascular exercise and is therefore considered good for rehabilitation.

The practice of pilates

The Pilates Method is a physical fitness system and Pilates called the method 'The Art of Contrology', which refers to the way the method encourages the use of the mind to control the muscles. This method represents a unique approach to exercise, that develops body awareness, improving and changing the body's postural and alignment habits and increasing flexibility and ease of movement. The methods of teaching pilates come from a core understanding of the anatomy of the body.

Pilates and the elderly

Pilates is particularly beneficial to the elderly because it improves general fitness, helping to increase and create a balance between strength and flexibility. It also improves coordination, relieves stress and anxiety and helps the balance of the body by improving posture. Pilates exercises teach awareness of neutral alignment of the spine and help strengthen the deep postural muscles that support this alignment, which are important to help alleviate and prevent back pain.

T'ai chi

T'ai chi (pronounced tie chee) is an ancient Chinese discipline that integrates mind, body and spirit. Practitioners use meditation and deep breathing as they move through a series of continuous exercises. These exercises are called 'forms' which resemble slow-moving ballet. Though it originated as a martial art, t'ai chi is now practised more for its therapeutic benefits which include reducing stress, promoting balance and flexibility, and even easing pain from arthritis.

T'ai chi for the elderly

For hundreds of years, groups of Chinese people – many of them elderly – have performed t'ai chi's fluid, graceful movements in parks throughout China as a way of staying strong. Today, many people in the United States, Canada and Europe have become interested in attaining the health benefits of this ancient art as well. T'ai chi, practised on a regular basis, can increase stamina, strength and flexibility. It can also help with chronic pain and is believed to help slow the onset and progress of many forms of degenerative disease. It helps with arthritis, by strengthening the muscles surrounding an arthritic joint and improving flexibility, but it cannot replace loss of cartilage. It is known to improve balance which is particularly useful for older people as they are more prone to falls which can lead to serious complications. It is also good for circulation and high blood pressure. T'ai chi generally increases the range of motion without causing pain. T'ai chi is also a form of physical meditation, providing release from stress and leading to a sense of peace and emotional well being. T'ai chi can be used as a preventive health measure, as a way to maintain good health or to help with a specific ailment. Whilst t'ai chi cannot cure disease, it is often recommended as a complementary therapy to conventional treatment.

How it works

T'ai chi benefits the entire body, increasing muscle strength and enhancing balance and flexibility. People who practice t'ai chi are also said to exploit the strength of Yin (the earth) and the energy of Yang (the heavens) through exercises designed to express these forces in balanced and harmonious form. You will be taught to focus on your 'Dantian', an area in the lower abdomen just beneath the navel, which is the body's centre of gravity. This will help you relax and centre yourself. Deep breathing (from the diaphragm as opposed to the chest) is a key element of t'ai chi. You will learn to co-ordinate your breathing with each movement you make. Sessions typically start with some sort of meditation to calm the mind, followed by easy warm-up exercises to get the blood circulating.

Is it safe?

T'ai chi is safe for people of all ages and fitness levels. However, if you are older and sedentary, consult your doctor before starting t'ai chi and always inform your instructor of any medical conditions. As with yoga, you should not feel any discomfort or aches and pains with t'ai chi. If you do, tell your instructor who will modify the exercises accordingly.

How do I learn It?

Researchers say even though t'ai chi is one of the safest exercises around, elderly people interested in being taught should seek out a class designed for older adults and talk with a doctor before starting a programme. Alternatively you can teach yourself from books, videos and DVDs although you will miss out on feedback and class participation. You need to wear comfortable clothes and t'ai chi can be done in shoes or bare feet. For more information visit www.thehealthierlife.co.uk or www.classicaltaichi.com. To purchase books on t'ai chi try www.taichi4seniors.com.

SUMMARY

There are many forms of exercise to choose from and it is up to you which you fancy. The most important thing is to do something otherwise you will most definitely put on weight and lose flexibility. Even if you hate the thought of exercise, putting it into practice is often not as arduous as you might think. You are not trying to perform in the Olympics after all, but you do want to be independent and able to enjoy your life without being compromised by ill health. Obviously, there are some health issues that cannot be addressed through exercise, but it follows that if you do nothing during your retirement and become a couch potato, you will only have yourself to blame for a poor quality of life. Remember exercise does not have to cost money . . . walking is free!

DIET

Most peoples' diet can be improved just by cutting down on fats, salt and sugar. However, there are many other important aspects of diet to consider as well, such as:

- Are you getting enough fruit and vegetables?
- Is there enough fibre in your diet?
- Are you eating too many carbohydrates?
- How often do you eat junk food?
- Are you overweight?
- Are you drinking too much alcohol?

THE BASICS

There are so many aspects to diet that this section of the book can only cover the basics of what is believed to be good for you and what isn't. There are many different diets on the market which are not just for losing weight but for improving your health and lifestyle. These diets depend on the needs of the individual. There are also dieticians who can give you advice on a diet that fits your personal needs.

Being overweight

Being overweight carries many health risks including heart disease, high blood pressure, diabetes, breathing difficulties and some cancers. It also leads to lethargy, brought about through lack of energy and depression. There is no two ways about it: being overweight is bad for you and can reduce your life expectancy. Obesity causes on average the deaths of 9,000 people per year in England alone! Those with a serious weight problem should consult their GP for advice. They may prescribe medication or refer you to a dietician. Some GPs can offer vouchers or discounts to exercise sessions. So, if you want a healthier and longer life, you will have to watch what you eat.

Exercise and healthy eating

The best way to lose weight is through exercise and eating a healthy diet. This means eating fresh food daily and cutting down on junk food which can be high in sugar and fat content.

Fruit and vegetables

Fruit and vegetables are necessary for a healthy diet and you should eat at least five portions a day. Eating a variety of fruit and vegetables will give you plenty of vitamins and minerals as many are high in folic acid and vitamin C. Fruit and vegetables are also a good source of fibre and antioxidants which are necessary nutrients for your health. They are also:

◆ Low in fat.
◆ Low in calories.
◆ Contain no added sugars.
◆ Can reduce the risk of heart disease.
◆ Can reduce the risk of some cancers.

Smoothies

If you don't like eating fruit, you could try blending it with fruit juice to make a 'smoothie'. Bananas are particularly good for this.

The five a day portion indicator

On some food packets you may see a 'five a day portion indicator'. This shows you how many portions of fruit or vegetables the serving of food contains. The five a day portion indicator will help you choose a diet with plenty of different fruit and vegetables, however, not all foods carry the logo as they may not meet the criteria.

Easy ways to get the five a day into your diet

◆ Chop up dried fruit and add it to your cereal.
◆ Snack on pieces of fruit or vegetables.
◆ Add a portion of salad to sandwiches or serve it with your main meal of the day.
◆ Be adventurous with vegetables, there are so many different ways to cook them and don't be afraid of trying something new.
◆ Tinned fruit can be added to puddings, but try and avoid those in syrup as they contain a lot of sugar.

Cooking vegetables

Vegetables should not be overcooked. They are at their most delicious and nutritious when they are 'al dente', which is slightly crunchy. If you want to add extra flavour to vegetables, you could try adding lemon juice, garlic or spices such as ginger.

Drinking juice

No matter how much fruit juice you drink, it will only count as one portion of the five a day portion plan.

Fresh, frozen, chilled or canned

The fruit and vegetables contained in convenience foods, soups and puddings can contribute to the five a day portion plan. The downside to convenience foods is that they can contain a lot of salt, sugar and fat. Always check the nutritional information on the label and if the writing is too small to read . . . take your glasses!

Breakfast

A lot of people skip breakfast or maybe just grab a cup of coffee, but avoiding breakfast is a mistake. This meal helps kick start your day and boosts your metabolism. Some people believe (wrongly) that avoiding breakfast will help them lose weight, but this theory is misguided as they will most likely do more 'snacking' during the day. Many breakfast cereals are a good source of nutrients and fibre, which help improve bowel health. Many cereals, however, do have a high sugar and salt content, so do check the label. Porridge is a good way to start the day as the oats help reduce cholesterol levels. Add some fresh or dried fruit to your cereal, as this will be part of the five a day portion plan.

Cholesterol

Cholesterol is produced by the liver and is a waxy, fat-like substance. Although cholesterol is often thought of as a 'bad thing', the truth is that cholesterol also has purposes important to your overall health and body function. Every cell within the body is formed, to varying degrees, from cholesterol and at appropriate levels, cholesterol plays a vital role in many functions of the body.

High cholesterol

High cholesterol dramatically increases your chances of having a heart attack or stroke resulting in paralysis, brain damage and even death. It is a leading cause of heart disease and clogged arteries. Untreated, it can cause severe health problems including stroke, kidney damage, blindness and heart attacks. On average, people with uncontrolled high cholesterol are more likely to have a heart attack, develop congestive heart failure or have a stroke.

How to reduce high cholesterol

When the cholesterol levels become high, it can be dangerous. Cholesterol levels begin to increase with age, with men generally developing high cholesterol levels earlier. Your genetic make up will play a part too. If your parents have a history of coronary heart disease, the chances are that you may too. However, there are ways you can help reduce your cholesterol levels through diet and lifestyle such as:

◆ Reduce consumption of foods high in animal saturated fats.
◆ Being overweight increases the level of 'bad' cholesterol, so you will need to try and lose weight in order to reduce it.
◆ Take exercise, as regular exercising helps lower cholesterol and keeps your body functioning well.
◆ Smoking, too much alcohol and stress are all linked to high cholesterol.

Salt

Too much salt can cause high blood pressure which can increase your risk of coronary heart disease and strokes. Consume no more than six grams (a teaspoon) of salt a day. A lot of the salt we eat today is 'hidden' in processed foods, takeaways, canned soups and ready meals. Look at the labels and choose foods low in salt. Salt is often listed as sodium on labels. One gram of sodium equals 2.5 grams of salt and always check the amount of salt per serving, not per 100 grams. Beware of crisps, which are particularly high in salt and always choose products which say 'no added salt'.

Sugar and carbohydrates

Carbohydrates are the compounds which provide energy to living cells. The carbohydrates we use as foods have their origin in the photosynthesis of plants. They take the form of sugars, starches and cellulose. The name carbohydrate means 'watered carbon' or carbon with attached water molecules.

Carbohydrates in diet

Our carbohydrate intake should come mainly from complex carbohydrates such as vegetables, fruits and grains, rather than the simple carbohydrates found in sugars. Complex carbohydrates add more fibre, vitamins and minerals to the diet than foods high in refined sugars. Foods high in complex carbohydrates are usually lower in calories, saturated fat and cholesterol. A recommended intake is 20–30 grams of fibre a day.

Which foods are sources of complex carbohydrates?

- **Starches:** flour, bread, rice, corn, oats, barley, potatoes, fruits and vegetables.
- **Fibre-insoluble:** whole-wheat breads and cereals, wheat bran, cabbage, beets, carrots, brussel sprouts, turnips, cauliflower and apple peel.
- **Fibre-soluble:** oat bran, oats, citrus fruits, strawberries, apple pulp, rice, bran and barley.

Which foods are sources of simple carbohydrates?

- **Sucrose:** table sugar, brown sugar, confectioner's sugar, raw sugar.
- **Glucose:** corn syrup and glucose syrup.
- **Fructose:** fruits, vegetables and honey.
- **High fructose:** liquid sweetener that contains 42–90% fructose.
- **Honey:** made up of glucose, fructose and water.
- **Lactose:** milk and milk products.

How much complex carbohydrate should I eat?

People should eat at least five servings of fruits and vegetables a day (see the five a day portion plan) and 20–30 grams of fibre.

Coffee

Approximately 70 million cups of coffee are consumed everyday within the UK. Research has suggested that drinking four to five cups of coffee a day is perfectly safe for adults. These recommendations are based on the average amount of caffeine in cups of coffee, but this obviously can vary dependent on the strength of coffee you prefer. Although caffeine is a mild diuretic, drinking a moderate amount of coffee is unlikely to have a diuretic affect on the body. Coffee can contribute to your daily fluid intake and is a good source of antioxidants in comparison to tea and fruit juice. It is thought that antioxidants can protect the cells in the body from damage.

How much water/fluids should I drink a day?

How much water you need depends on many factors including your health status, how active you are and where you live. Water is crucial to your health. It makes up, on average, 60% of your body weight. Every system in your body depends on water. Lack of water can lead to dehydration. Even mild dehydration can sap your energy and make you tired. Dehydration poses a particular health risk for the very young and the very old. Signs and symptoms of dehydration include:

◆ Excessive thirst.
◆ Fatigue.
◆ Headache, lightheadedness or dizziness.
◆ Dry mouth.
◆ Little or no urination.
◆ Muscle weakness.

How much water do you need?

Every day you lose water through sweating, exhaling, urinating and bowel movements. For your body to function properly, you need to replace this water by consuming beverages and foods that contain water. The average urine output for adults is 1.5 litres a day. You lose close to an additional litre of water a day through breathing, sweating and bowel movements. Food usually accounts for 20% of your fluid intake, so you if you consume 2 litres of water or other beverages a day (a little more than 8 cups), along with your normal diet, you can replace the lost fluids.

Alcohol

Excessive drinking can damage the liver, heart and cause serious mental health problems. It is also linked with various cancers including breast, throat and mouth cancer. Alcohol is also connected to high blood pressure. Some alcohol, however, can be good for you, but only in moderation. Stick within the guidelines of safe drinking and avoid binge drinking or drinking on medication.

Government guidelines on safe drinking
- Three to four units of alcohol per day for men.
- Two to three units of alcohol per day for women.

However, some medical experts believe these levels are too high, and recommend no more than three units a day for men and two a day for women. The reason that the limits for women are less than for men is because the body composition of women has less water than men. Therefore, even if a man and woman are of similar size and weight, the woman will tend to get drunk faster. Women can also develop liver disease at lower levels of drinking than men.

What is a unit?

One unit is equivalent to:

- About half a pint (300ml) of ordinary strength lager, beer or cider.
- A 25ml pub measure of spirit or a small glass of fortified wine, such as sherry or port (17.5% ABV).
- A small glass (125 ml) of 8% ABV wine.

What is ABV?

The strength of an alcoholic drink is indicated by the percentage of alcohol by volume (ABV). A unit is 8 grams of pure alcohol, regardless of the amount of liquid it's contained in. The number of units in one litre of any drink is equal to the ABV. Therefore, a 500ml can of 8% ABV lager contains 4 units.

Problem drinkers

If you suspect you have a problem with drink, contact the organisation of Alcoholics Anonymous, which is free to anyone who suspects they may have a drink problem. Don't assume that problem drinkers are all down at heel drop outs – far from it. Some of the most respected members of society have had a problem with drink ... even George Bush is a reformed drinker. Whether you like him or not, you've got to admit that being the president of the USA is a pretty powerful position to be in, and hardly fits within the stereotypical image of an alcoholic – a park bench drunk! You can contact Alcoholics Anonymous on 0845 769 7555.

Smoking

Everyone on this planet apart from babies must know that smoking is bad for you. So all I will say here is that if you want help to quit then call the NHS Smoking Helpline on 0800 1690 169 for advice and help on giving up.

Getting a flu jab

It is wise, if you are aged 65 or over, to get a flu jab. Although anyone can get flu, it can be more serious for those who have reached 65 or over. Even if you feel fit and healthy, a bout of flu could lead to more serious problems, such as bronchitis or pneumonia which can lead to hospitalisation. The best time to have a flu jab is between September and early November before the 'flu season' starts. The vaccine offers protection for about a year and, although it cannot guarantee that you will not get flu, it greatly reduces the chances and the severity of the attack if you do. You may also be offered the 'pneumo jab' which helps protect you against pneumococcal infection. This is a 'one-off' jab that need not be repeated and it can be given at the same time as the flu jab. Contact your local GP for details.

Useful health organisations
- The Stroke Association: 0208 99422847 or visit www.stroke.org.uk.
- Osteoporosis: 0845 450 0230 or visit www.nos.org.uk.
- Cancer: 0808 800 1234 or visit www.cancerbacup.org.uk.
- Diabetes UK: 0845 120 2960 or visit www.diabetes.org.uk.
- Heart: 0870 600 6566 or visit www.bhf.org.uk.

Looking good
The motto here is: don't let yourself go! Just because you are getting older doesn't meant that you should let your standards slip and walk around looking a mess. You should, if anything, pay more attention to your appearance than you did when you were younger. Let's face it, it's easy to look good when you are young and fresh faced, and much harder when everything is beginning to droop and sag. Remember, you can still feel good about yourself even if you no longer look like a super model! It's just a question of taking pride in your appearance and making the best of yourself. If you look good, the chances are you will feel good. So, if you have let yourself go, male or female, go and get your hair cut or styled, lose weight and treat yourself to some new clothes . . . you'll feel ten years younger!

SUMMARY
What is obvious is that if you want to give your health the best chance you can, you will have to pay attention to diet, exercise and lifestyle. Of course, there are no guarantees that if you follow the rules you will live a long and happy life, but at least it gives you more of a sporting chance in life's lottery. There is no doubt that the more we learn about what is good for us, coupled with the breakthroughs in modern medicine, the longer we can expect to live.

7

Finance

The big question for retirees and potential retirees is can you afford to retire? It's all very well having dreams of what you are going to do when you finally give up work, but most of these plans involve some expense. With the loss of one or two incomes you will need to do the maths. This will be time consuming and tedious, but has to be done thoroughly so that you can get an accurate picture. The government estimates life expectancy as being 84 for men and 87 for women. That's a long time to provide for yourself, even if you retire at the standard age of 65. Therefore, it's important to get your sums right.

OCCUPATIONAL PENSION

You can begin drawing your occupational pension from the age of 50 (from 2010 this will rise to 55), whether you have actually given up working or not.

FINAL SALARY SCHEME

If you are lucky enough to be on a final salary scheme it is worth hanging on to get a pay rise? Or being made redundant? Or should you continue working on a part time/freelance basis? The dangers of jumping too early can be offset by the fear of delaying too late, so that mobility and health issues get in the way.

PRE-RETIREMENT PLANNING

For pre-retirement planning you can consult the Pre-Retirement Association (PRA) tel: 01483 301170 or visit www.pra.uk.com.

WHAT AM I ENTITLED TO?

The Financial Services Authority, the independent watchdog set up by the government to regulate the financial services industry, has published a full range of factsheets which are worth consulting. They cover all topics ranging from pensions and annuities to choosing a financial adviser and will help you through this difficult terrain. This chapter can only give you an introduction to this subject and you should consult a professional regarding your specific circumstances. Tel: 0845 606 1234 or visit www.fsa.gov.uk for more information.

How to choose the right financial adviser

Choosing the right financial adviser is obviously crucial. You should only go to a reputable company that is well established and approved by the FSA. Don't go to the cheapest or a 'friend of a friend'. We are talking about your hard earned savings here and the arrangements that you will need to make to provide for your old age.

'Keyfacts'

An FSA approved adviser will give you a document, with a 'Keyfacts' symbol, laying out the service the firm is offering, the cost of these services and whether you will pay by fee or commission. Obviously it is worth shopping around to compare approaches, costs and who you think is most in tune with your needs. The Institute of Financial Planning has a national register of fee-based financial planners. Tel: 0117 945 2470 or visit www.financialplanning.org.uk.

WHAT PENSIONS HAVE YOU GOT?

Regarding personal, stakeholder and occupation pensions you will need to talk to your pension adviser or the trustees and scheme administrator to find out what your pension is worth. They pay your pension to you in a variety of different ways:

- If you have a personal or stakeholder pension you will have to buy an annuity with your fund, which is used to provide income withdrawal. You can take a quarter of the fund as a tax free lump sum before buying an annuity.
- Occupation salary related schemes pay the pension directly to you. Usually you can take part of the fund as a tax free lump sum.
- Occupation schemes used to buy an annuity on your behalf, but from April 2006 you may be able to shop around yourself. Again, you can take out a cash lump sum before buying an annuity.
- From April 2006 you will also be able to draw a pension from your employer's occupational pension scheme and carry on working for that employer, subject to the rules of the scheme.
- If your total pension pot is worth less than £15,000 you can convert the full amount into a cash lump sum, tax free from April 2006.
- If you have changed employers in the past, you can find out what has happened to old pension entitlements by contacting the Pension Scheme Registry tel: 0191 225 6393 or visit www.thepensions regulator.gov.uk.

Tracing old pensions and life policies

To trace old pensions call the Pension Tracing Service on tel: 0845 600 2537 or visit www.thepensionservice.gov.uk. To trace life policies, shares and other financial assets contact The Unclaimed Assets Register on tel: 0870 241 1713 or visit www.uar.co.uk. Another useful number is for The Pensions Advisery Service, tel: 0845 601 2923 or visit www.pensionsadviseryservice.org.uk. This is an independent organisation providing help with consumers' pension and annuity queries.

WHAT IS AN ANNUITY?

This converts your pension fund into an investment fund that will pay you an income for the rest of your life – however long you live. You purchase the annuity from an insurance company and the income is taxable. The amount you receive will depend on the scheme that you are in. Some are better than others as they are affected by interest rates and how the average life span is calculated. You need to buy an annuity if you have a personal or stakeholder pension, additional voluntary contributions, free standing additional voluntary contributions, retirement annuity contracts or a Section 32 policy. Previously you would have to buy an annuity before you reached 75 years of age, but from April 2006 you can draw an income from an alternatively secured pension fund instead. There is a maximum level of income that can be withdrawn, but not a minimum, and it is likely to be applicable for those with funds over £100,000 or additional sources of income.

What types of annuities are there?

- **Single Life:** if you don't have a partner or spouse.
- **Joint Life:** pays out to your partner or spouse after your death.
- **Level Annuity:** which pays the same amount each year.
- **Escalating Annuity:** the amount increases each year – either by a fixed rate or linked to the Retail Price Index.

You can choose an annuity that guarantees to pay out for a minimum period of five or ten years.

Comparisons

The FSA runs a comparison service so that you can compare the rates that you are quoted to see where they fall in the bandwidth of payments per month. The rates for a man aged 65 with a £50,000 single life annuity range from £262 to £304 a month, so it is worth checking it out on their comparative tables.

The rights of ex-spouses

In some recent divorce cases, a share of the pension scheme has been granted. The law takes into account the fact that a spouse is still deemed to have contributed even if they have not been earning.

STATE PENSION

If you have been paying National Insurance Contributions (NICs) for at least 10 or 11 years, you will get an occupational pension from the age of 65 for men and 60 for women (this will increase to 65 in 2010). The longer you have contributed the more you will get. This is an immediate problem for women, only 16% of whom qualify for the full state pension because of gaps in their contributions, due to care responsibilities. The Pension Service should get in touch with you three months before you are due to claim a pension. If they don't, tel: 0845 300 1084/0845 60 60 265 or visit www.thepensionservice.gov.uk.

Deferment

Postpone claiming your pension and you get 10% extra for each year that you don't claim, or a one-off lump sum on what you have not claimed, plus 2% above base rate. If you want to defer, contact the Pension Service via their website (www.the pensionservice.gov.uk) or tel: 08457 31 32 32. Additionally, when you have passed the pension age and continue working, you stop paying National Insurance contributions on your earnings.

State Earnings Related Pension Scheme (SERPS)

Since 1978 employees automatically build up an additional state pension, unless they specifically contracted out. This was known as SERPS but is now called the State Second Pension. It is unavailable to the self employed.

Pension forecast

The Pension Service runs a forecasting service which will enable you to ascertain what your future state pension will be. Visit the pension website as before or tel: 0845 3000 169.

Pension credit

In order to help pensioners with little or no savings, the government guarantees an income of at least £109 a week if you are single and aged 60 to 64. If you are over 65 then it is currently £155 per week. For couples aged 60 to 64 it's £167 per week, or over 65 it is currently £221 per week. If your income is higher than this you can still get Penson Credit if you are:

♦ Severely disabled.
♦ Looking after someone who is severely disabled.
♦ Have certain housing costs such as mortgage payments.

For advice and information tel: 0800 99 1234.

Extra entitlements

♦ **Age related payments:** £200 for people over 65 for help with council tax – if you don't get the guaranteed element of pension credit. This should be paid directly to you before Christmas.

- **Winter fuel payment:** paid directly to you before Christmas. If you haven't received the payment in the past, tel: 029 2042 8106 to find out if you are eligible.
- **Over 70's £50 payment:** again, this is paid to you before Christmas, if you receive the guaranteed element of Pension Credit.
- **Housing and council tax benefit:** if you claim Pension Credit, you should have completed the relevant form. If not contact your local council, social security office or the Pension Service.
- **Community care grants:** this provides financial help to buy items such as furniture, cooker, carpets, bed and bedding. Or in cases where you need help to stay at home, return home from a place where you have been getting care, ease exceptional pressure on your family or care for a prisoner or young offender released from custody.
- **Funeral payment:** this covers the cost of burial or cremation fees and up to £700 for other costs such as coffins or flowers. This may be available if you are claiming pension credit, or housing benefit and can cover a close relative or friend. The amount is dependant on the value of the assets of the deceased. Claim forms are available from the Pension Service, Jobcentre or social security office.
- **Bereavement payments:** if you are over the state pension age and receiving a pension you will not be eligible for this. However, if your husband or wife has paid sufficient National Insurance Contributions and has not received a state pension you may be eligible for up to £2,000. Claims can be made up to 12 months after death and forms can be obtained from the Pension Service, Jobcentre or your local social security office.
- **Budgeting loans from the social fund:** these are one-off, interest free loans if you have been getting pension credit, income support or jobseeker's allowance for at least 26 weeks. Contact the Pension Service, Jobcentre or your social security office.

- **Crisis loans from the social fund:** an interest free loan to get you through an emergency. Contact the Pension Service, Jobcentre or your local social security office.
- **Living abroad** – Contact the Pensions Service to find out which countries are covered and how the government pays pensions and benefits to people living abroad.
- **Attendance allowance** – If you are over 65 and have needed help looking after yourself for at least six months, you can claim for personal care. This is not means tested and has a middle and higher rating of payment. For advice and information tel: 0800 88 22 00.
- **Carers allowance** – You can claim if you earn less than £82 a week, are not in full time education and look after a severely disabled person for at least 35 hours a week. The disabled person must be claiming: Attendance Allowance, middle or highest rate with Disability Living Allowance or Constant Attendance Allowance. If you receive a pension and some benefits this may affect whether you can claim this allowance. For advice and information tel: 01253 856 123.
- **War disablement pension:** if you have been injured or disabled in a war ring the Veterans Agency: tel: 0800 169 2277 or visit www.veteransagency.mod.uk.
- **War widows' or widowers' pension:** if your husband or wife was killed in the armed forces you should contact the Veterans Agency as above. They may help with funeral expenses. This pension may be withdrawn if you remarry or live with a new partner – but it could start again if that relationship ends!

What you get for free!

- **Travel:** if you are over 60 you are entitled to a bus pass, which allows you at least half price bus fares (see Travel, Chapter 3).
- **Passports:** if you were born before 2nd September 1929 you are entitled to a free ten year passport. For more information tel: 0870 521 0410.

- **Driving licence:** once you reach 70 you can apply for a free three year driving licence. To find out more information, tel: 0870 240 0009.
- **TV licences:** these are free to anyone aged 75 or over. For further information tel: 0845 603 6999 or visit www.tvlicensing.co.uk.
- **Admission to museums and galleries:** most are free admission, but some still charge. Tel: 0207 211 6200 or visit www.culture.gov.uk to check which museums and galleries charge.

INHERITANCE TAX (IHT)

The Inland Revenue has got many IHT avoidance schemes in its sights so it probably isn't worth all the time and expense in setting up complicated trusts and other schemes.

- Any estate currently worth more than £275,000 is taxed at 40%.
- IHT is not payable when an estate is passed between married couples. When the survivor dies the whole estate is taxed, unless the couple have set up a trust that safeguards both at nil rate bands of £275,000. This is easily done and should be included in your will.

WILLS

If you don't make a will this will lead to all manner of problems and cause chaos for your descendants. The winners in this case are the lawyers and the state. Will forms can be obtained from the post office, but it is safer to get a solicitor to draw one up and let your family know where it is kept. Age Concern or the Citizens Advice Bureau can help you with this.

The art of 'Spending the Kids' Inheritance' by giving it to them now!

The art of good financial planning is to try and keep most of your hard earned cash out of the clutches of the taxman. So, it might be a more productive plan to give your kids as much of their inheritance as you can during your lifetime. Depending on their circumstances, the kids could probably put it to better use sooner, rather than later. They might need financial help buying their first home, having a baby, paying for schooling, a car or even having a really good holiday. You also get the pleasure of seeing them putting their inheritance to good use, rather than have it gather dust in stocks and shares or a bank account. It also removes the money from your estate and ultimately out of the taxman's hands, so it makes good financial sense.

- You can make gifts of £3,000 free of IHT or £6,000 if you did not make a gift the previous year.
- You can give £250 to as many people as you want each year.
- You can give £5,000 to a child that is getting married. Any other relative can give £2,500 and friends £1,000.
- Gifts to political parties and charities are tax free.
- Cash given to a relative or friend, as long as you do not die for seven years, is tax free. If you die three to four years after the gift, IHT is reduced by 20%, four to five years by 40%, five to six years 60%, six to seven years 80%.

INCOME TAX ALLOWANCES

You still have to pay taxes on your pension, state pension and carer's allowance, but your allowances do increase slightly. Currently they are:

- Between 65 and 74 you get an age related personal allowance on earnings of £7,090.
- Over 75 this increases to £7,220.
- Married couples allowance between 70 and 74 is £5,905, over 75 it is £5,975.
- If one partner is working, make sure that any income bearing accounts or investments are held in the other partner's name.

RENTING OUT A ROOM IN YOUR HOUSE

You won't pay tax on the first £4,250 of rental income from renting out a room in your house. Make sure you have a proper agreement and check references. Any income above this amount will be treated for tax in the normal way. You can check out all the details on www.direct.gov.uk.

CAPITAL GAINS TAX (CGT)

CGT is payable if you make a profit on the sale of a capital asset over and above your capital gains tax allowance, which is currently £8,500 per person per year. It increases annually in the Budget but does not increase with age. As a married couple you can aggregate both allowances together, if the asset is held in joint names. The rate thereafter, is dependent on your income. A higher rate tax payer will pay 40%. If you have no taxable income the rates will be calculated as follows:

◆ The first £2,090   10%
◆ The next £32,400   20%
◆ Thereafter   40%

TAX FREE ALLOWANCES

If you are a married couple, try to make sure you are both using all of your tax allowances. Assets can be transferred, tax free, from one partner to another.

◆ If one of you has made a capital gain of more than £8,500 on a sale during the financial year and you want to sell another asset, transfer the money into your spouse's name to avoid CGT.
◆ If you are working, the rate of CGT is the same as your income tax rate. So, again, if you are paying 40% and your partner is on the basic rate it's worth doing the sums.
◆ You do not pay CGT on the sale of your home, your car, PEPs, government bonds, betting, lottery or pool winnings and personal belongings up to £6,000.

- You cannot give assets to your children, family, friends or sell them assets for less than their true worth, without having to consider CGT.
- If you make a capital loss you may be able to make a claim to deduct that loss from other capital gains – but only if that asset normally attracts CGT.
- If someone dies and leaves their belongings to their beneficiaries, there is no CGT to pay at that time. However, if an asset is later disposed of by a beneficiary, any CGT they may have to pay will be based on the difference between the market value at the time of death and the value at the time of disposal.

TAPER RELIEF

From April 1998 Taper Relief was introduced for assets that have been held over a period of time. Residential property, apart from your own home, is classed as a 'non-business asset' so qualifies on a fixed annual rate as follows:

- Property held for less than 3 years   Nil
- Property held for 3 years but less than 4   5%
- Property held for 4 years but less than 5   10%
- Property held for 5 years but less than 6   15%
- Property held for 6 years but less than 7   20%
- Property held for 7 years but less than 8   25%
- Property held for 8 years but less than 9   30%
- Property held for 9 years but less than 10   35%
- Property held for 10 years or more   40%

If you held the property from before 17th March 1998, you are allowed to add an extra year onto the above formula.

HOW TO GET YOUR HANDS ON SOME MONEY

People who own their own homes are at an immediate advantage over those that do not, as there is a store of untapped cash locked away in the value of their house. You have two options:

- You can sell your home.
- Stay put and raise money through an equity release scheme.

If you want to sell

Obviously if you want to move, downsize or live abroad then selling is the best option and you can do it in the normal way. However, if you need to move quickly because long term care is required, for example, there are companies that specialise in quick sales. This means exactly what it says. They will buy the house from you without you having to wait for it to sell but this will be at a discounted price of approximately 20% off the market value of the house. They make their money on the eventual sale price of the house. It's expensive and it's important to check the company out, but if you have a house that is just not selling, you might feel that it is worth paying the price to avoid any stress and aggravation.

If you want to stay put

There are two types of scheme to release the equity in your house:

- Lifetime mortgages.
- Home reversions.

You can apply for these schemes if you own your property freehold or leasehold and have paid most of the mortgage off. The property should be worth a minimum of £50,000 and you must be over 55 years old. Some schemes are only available for those over 65 or even 70. Useful advice is available from:

- Age Concern publishes a guide called *Using your home as Capital*. Tel: 0800 00 99 66 or visit www.ace.org.uk.
- Help the Aged Equity Release give advice on the most appropriate equity release scheme for your needs. Tel: 0845 2300 820 or visit www.helptheaged.org.uk/equityrelease.
- The Financial Service Authority consumer helpline can be contacted on tel: 0845 606 1234 or visit www.fsa.gov.uk.
- Moneyfacts Publications can be contacted on tel: 0870 2250 100 or visit www.moneyfacts.co.uk.

Lifetime mortgages

Basically you are raising a loan, from a bank or building society, against the value of your home. As such, you still own your home. You will be able to live in it for life and if you take out the equity release scheme in joint names, the mortgage will continue until the second one of you dies. Generally you will not be able to borrow more than 50% of the value of your home. It is usually best to get a fixed rate loan so that you are not at the mercy of upward rising interest rates.

No negative equity guarantee

It is important to check that there is a 'no negative equity' guarantee so that you never owe more than the property is worth. If you want to move and sell your home, check that this is allowed. Also, check that if you move to a cheaper home and want to repay part of the loan you will not be penalised for doing so. Again, get yourself a good financial adviser. There are different ways to receive the money:

- You can take a cash lump sum. This lump sum can be re-invested in an annuity or another type of investment that will pay you a regular income.
- You can take money out on a drawdown basis – when you want it. This means that you are only borrowing the money when you actually need it. This will probably cost you less, as the rate of interest

charged by the mortgage company will be more than you make from your annuity or investments.

Similarly there are different ways that you can pay for the use of the money:

+ Interest only mortgage: you can pay the monthly interest from the loan. It is best to get a fixed rate to guard against upward fluctuations. The amount you borrowed is repaid when you sell your home.
+ Roll up mortgage: you do not pay the interest on the loan until your house has been sold. The amount you borrow may have been relatively small but with the interest added to the loan and compounded, the size of the loan can grow quite considerably over the years.
+ Fixed repayment lifetime mortgage: instead of being charged interest, you pay an agreed figure. The amount you will have to pay back will be negotiated before you take out the loan and will be dependant on your age and life expectancy.

Care and repair and staying put schemes

If you need some money to pay for home improvements or to adapt your home, there is a non-profit making organisation called the Home Improvement Trust. A scheme called 'Houseproud' has been set up which acts as an 'impartial go-between' to liaise with the bank or building society and arrange valuations. It arranges for you to get free advice from an independent financial adviser. They then work with the home improvement agencies to get advice, supervise repairs, improvements and adaptations to your home. The Home Improvement Trust can be contacted on tel: 0800 783 7569 or visit www.improvement trust.fsbusiness.co.uk (see Chapter 14 on Staying Put or Moving On).

HOME REVERSIONS

This works differently to the mortgage in that you sell all, or part of your home to the lender. You can get a cash lump sum or an annuity but you will have to sign a lease to live in the property, as a tenant for the rest of your life (or until you no longer need it). Again, if the scheme is done in joint names the mortgage will continue until both partners are deceased.

How home reversions work

The minimum age for these schemes is higher than for a lifetime mortgage as the buyer cannot sell the property until after your death or you have moved into a care home.

♦ You will not get the full market value of your property. Depending on your age and sex, you will only be able to get about 35% to 60% of what your home is worth.

♦ When the property is sold, your estate only gets the benefit from the rise in the value of the unsold portion of the property. If you sold 100% your estate will receive nothing, if you sold 50%, the estate receive 50% of the increase in value of the property.

With this in mind it is vital that the valuation of your home is carried out properly and by an independent professional as this determines how much money you will get. You might also have to pay a nominal rent or not so nominal, if you want to raise additional money. The responsibility for repairs is still yours.

Equity release plans: the advantages

♦ You don't have to move house to raise extra cash.

♦ The money released is tax free.

♦ You can get a lump sum or regular income.

♦ You can reduce inheritance tax by giving the money away (covered earlier in the chapter).

♦ You can pay for care bills, should they be required.

Equity release plans: the disadvantages

- Interest rates are higher than ordinary mortgages.
- There is a reduction in what you will leave in your estate.
- You may lose some social security benefits because of the additional income.

SAFE HOME INCOME PLAN (SHIP)

Since 1991 leading providers of equity release plans have observed the SHIP code of practice: 'It is dedicated entirely to the protection of plan holders and promotion of safe home income and equity release plans'. The trade body handles complaints and its members are regulated by the Financial Services Association. SHIP was formed as there were some schemes operating variable rate mortgages linked to investment bonds. Unfortunately the variable rates rose, house values fell and the investment returns did not cover the mortgage repayments which left some pensioners in dire straits.

Safety check

SHIP has issued a safety check on all schemes:

- Do I have the right to live in my property for life?
- Do I have the freedom to move to a suitable alternative property without financial penalties?
- Will I receive either a cash sum or regular income payments?

As a further safeguard your own solicitor, who will oversee the transaction on your behalf, must sign a certificate to acknowledge that the essential features and implications of your chosen SHIP have been brought to your attention. No SHIP member will ever attempt to sell you a scheme involving variable interest rates, as although they may look attractive, they can soon become a financial burden in unfavourable market conditions. This code has also been welcomed by Age Concern. To contact SHIP tel: 0870 241 6060 or visit www.ship-ltd.org.

Before you take out an equity release scheme

If you are on a low income and are considering an equity release scheme to supplement your income, first check out what welfare benefit entitlements you can claim for.

◆ Age Concern operate a free advice line, contact Seniorline tel: 0808 800 6565.
◆ If you are in debt call the National Debtline on tel: 0808 808 4000 or the Consumer Credit Counselling Service on tel: 0800 138 1111.
◆ Grants or loans are sometimes available from your council.

SUMMARY

Before entering into one of these schemes the most important thing to do is really consider whether your home is the right one for your needs. Would you be better selling your home, moving to something smaller and more suitable, or look into retirement housing? Whatever you do, it is worth discussing it with your family, as it will have some bearing on what their inheritance will be, although if you are determined to 'Spend The Kids' Inheritance' this will be of little concern!

8

Special Treats

Special treats are a great way to 'Spend The Kids' Inheritance'. If you want to do something out of the ordinary, there are many exciting things you can do. Obviously anything luxuriously special is not going to be cheap, so these treats are meant as 'one offs' rather than everyday events. If you have a special anniversary, birthday or some other reason to celebrate, and you can afford it . . . then why not be extravagant once in a while?

TEA AT 'THE RITZ'

For a special treat, taking 'Tea at The Ritz' has to be one of them. It is a tradition that has always been associated with indulging oneself . . . and why not in retirement? The tea is served in the glorious Palm Court and there are several varieties of tea available as well as cucumber sandwiches, freshly baked scones with jam and clotted cream plus a selection of pastries. There are five sittings daily at 11:30am, 1:30pm, 3:30pm, 5:30pm and 7:30pm. As tea at The Ritz is very popular, booking at least six weeks in advance is advisable. I have to confess to having had tea at The Ritz only once, as a special treat. As with all luxuries, it does not come cheap but it is a rather nice thing to do. I once shared a friend's birthday celebration there and we all thoroughly enjoyed the occasion. Make sure that you are aware of the dress code as jeans and trainers will not be allowed. Tel: 0207 493 8181 or visit www.theritzlondon.com/tea for information and current prices.

THE ORIENT EXPRESS

The Orient Express 'where you travel back in time to a more gracious era' has to be in the top ten list of special treats. You do not, however, have to travel to Venice to enjoy the experience, although that is a special treat well worth exploring. There are day trips that you can enjoy that depart from Victoria and travel through the English countryside. You will be served a five course lunch with champagne, wine and liqueurs. Passengers can disembark from the train during the trip and the dress code is 'you cannot be over dressed!' There are many companies that offer trips on The Orient Express and it is a question of shopping around to get the best deals. For further information tel: 0845 077 2222 or www.orient-express.com; tel: 0870 750 5711 or visit www.thomascook.com; tel: 0870 050 0808 or visit www.expedia.co.uk; or www.ebay.com; or tel: 0870 444 2524 or visit www.buyagift.com. There are so many more websites to choose from.

A DAY AT THE RACES

There are many race courses located around the UK. A day at the races could be that special treat you are looking for if you want to celebrate with friends and family. Call: 0800 652 4899 or visit www.a-day-at-the-races.com for more information.

FANCY DRIVING A FERRARI?

If you have a bit of the boy/girl racer in you then this could be the perfect special treat, but be warned – driving one of the finest Italian sports cars does not come cheap. You can hire a self drive package for one or two days, where you either collect the car or have it delivered to your home address. The company will give you a full briefing on the car controls. Cars are subject to availability and there are restrictions. You may need to book two to three weeks in advance to avoid disappointment. Bad weather conditions could affect your booking. Tel: 0870 360 0360 or visit www.driveme.net for information.

RALLY DRIVING

A considerably cheaper option is rally driving. All you need to take part is a full manual driving licence. There are many courses available to choose from and, again, it's a case of shopping around to get the best deal. Tel: 0845 330 5115 or visit www.virginexperiencedays.co.uk. They offer to teach you how to handle a rally car on tarmac or loose surfaces and to cope with cornering at speed and braking. They also have the only fully equipped disabled rally driving school in the country.

HELICOPTER FLIGHTS

If you want a bird's eye view of the land in which we live, then a helicopter ride has got to be the ultimate. With its large windows and ability to hover slowly above points of interest, be it your own home or a famous landmark, a helicopter ride offers you fantastic views. Even if you are familiar with the landscape, seeing it from a helicopter will offer a different perspective from that which you are used to. Helicopter flights are available in various parts of the UK. You can not only travel in a helicopter, you can also have lessons in how to fly them in dual controlled helicopters. If you are really ambitious this could be the start towards a private pilot's licence, if that is your retirement dream. Most people, however, will be content to sit back and enjoy the amazing views on offer. It is a great way of celebrating with family and friends. Inclement weather conditions could affect your flight. There are many companies offering both lessons and flights such as www.helicopter-flights.co.uk or tel: 0870 360 0360, or visit www.treatme.net or tel: 01959 578 100 or visit www.intotheblue.co.uk.

I'M A CELEBRITY!

Stretch limousines are the ultimate way to travel in luxury and arrive in style. Whether you are planning a night on the town, enjoying a trip to the theatre or celebrating an anniversary, birthday or any other special occasion, travelling in a limousine (it is not necessarily as expensive as you might think, particularly if there are eight of you sharing the cost) can be a glamorous and fun way to travel to your destination. You can sit back, relax and enjoy a drink whilst listening to your favourite music. Some limousines have 'mood lighting' and 'star-gazer optic fibre mirrored ceilings'. There are many companies offering their limousines for hire and you will need to research what their special packages can offer. Three of the many companies offering their services are: tel: 01753 655 075 or visit www.stretchlimos.co.uk; or tel: 01268 515 779 or visit www.luxlimo.co.uk; or tel: 08500 831 669 or visit www.ultimatelimo.co.uk.

BIRDS OF PREY

If you have always fancied being up close and personal with a falcon or two, this extraordinary 'treat' could be what you are looking for. It is one of the many unusual events offered by www.intotheblue.co.uk, tel: 01959 578 100. They say:

You will be given a short introduction to the ancient art of falconry and some of the birds of prey and will have the opportunity to handle and fly up to six different species such as hawks, buzzards, owls, falcons, eagles and vultures. At the end of the encounter the participant will receive a souvenir photograph of themselves holding a bird of prey.

GONE TO THE DOGS

Going to the 'dog track' can be a great way of spending a special evening with friends. Dog racing is not expensive and you can enjoy a bet without losing the house! You can either go it alone, or book a package through a company such as www.thedoghouse.co.uk or tel: 0871 288 4092. Their normal package includes:

- Admission for two people.
- One race card.
- Two drinks vouchers.
- Two fast food vouchers.

Please note that this package is only available for evening meetings and may vary depending on the location. There are no bookings taken in December. A race meeting generally lasts for three hours, and there are various locations to choose from such as: London, Manchester, Oxford, Portsmouth, Birmingham, Sunderland and Newcastle-Upon-Tyne.

MESSING ABOUT ON THE RIVER

If you fancy having your anniversary on board a boat then www.thedog house.co.uk or tel: 0871 288 4092 offer a package called 'The Ultimate Romantic trip'. The itinerary is as follows:

You'll board at 11.30 am and journey off on a tour of the mouth of the River Dart, past all the pretty houses and the castles whilst sipping on Champagne and enjoying nibbles. You can relax in luxury while your skipper guides you up river to a mooring for you to enjoy your luxury hamper – which will include:

- Champagne/smoked salmon
- Local cheeses
- Cold local meats (cut from the bone)
- Salad with home-made dressing
- Variety of delicious fresh breads
- Lemon, mayonnaise, chutneys
- Patisserie, fresh teas and coffees

After dining you are taken to a waterside village where you may stroll or visit a traditional local pub before heading back to Dartmouth, listening to music of your choice.

This package is available on selected days only from April to October and is available in Dartmouth, Devon only. If this is too far for you to travel then it is worth checking with local companies near you to see whether they offer such a package.

DAD'S ARMY

The Bressingham Steam Museum, near Diss in Norfolk, has as well as the traditional attractions of museums and gardens 'The Dad's Army Experience' and the information provided is as follows:

The television series 'Dad's Army' ran from 1968 to 1977 with a total of 80 episodes. Today, repeats are still being shown over 30 years after the first episode was made. Some of the vehicles from Bressingham Steam Museum were used in the series. The exhibition consists of the Church Hall & Vicar's office, Frazer's Workshop & Funeral Directors, Mainwaring's Swallow Bank, Jones's Butcher shop, Post Office & Stores, Francis Cupis's printers and David Cooke toyshop. The Dinky toys in the toyshop are part of a collection on loan from Mr. David Cooke and the steam models are from the David Woof collection. The contents of the Post Office store, Church Hall and Vicar's office are mostly on loan from the Dad's Army Appreciation Society.

Tel: 01379 686 900 or visit www.bressingham.co.uk for information on all their attractions.

NATIONAL ATTRACTIONS

There are many national treasures and sites of historical interest to visit. www.daysoutguide.co.uk is a website from National Rail which gives details of attractions (some with a two for one deal) in London and the South East. Or visit www.daysout.co.uk which lists nearly 7,000 attractions throughout the whole of the UK. You should also contact your local train station for information and details of attractions in your area. Another useful website for what's on in your area is www.wherecawego.com.

Whale watching

This is a four day trip to the Bay of Biscay off the French Coast where there is an extraordinary diversity of sea life. From the deck of a five star vessel you will be able to watch the whales and dolphins cavort in their natural habitat. The trip also includes a short stopover in northern Spain and is available from tel: 07002 892 443 or visit www.next2noth ing.co.uk.

Wild animals

You do not need go on safari to experience wild animals close up. You can feed tigers by hand, shadow a lion keeper or feed the meercats. For further information contact tel: 0870 606 6666 or visit www.next2noth ing.co.uk or www.thanksdarling.com; these are just two of several companies offering these experiences.

Days out and 'The National Trust'

The National Trust is a charity that looks after forests, woods, fens, beaches, farmland, downs, moorland, islands, archaeological remains, castles, houses, nature reserves and villages. They are the custodians of 612,000 acres of countryside in England, Wales and Northern Ireland, plus 700 miles of coastline and over 200 buildings and gardens of special interest. There are many membership categories, including a special membership rate for the over 60s. Once you become a member, you will receive a comprehensive membership pack with information on all the National Trust attractions which you will be able to visit free of charge. The National Trust claims that with so many attractions on offer, you are never more than 40 minutes away from a National Trust experience. For details on how to become a member tel: 0870 458 4000 or visit www.nationaltrust.org.uk.

The spa experience at Champneys

There are now many health clubs situated around the UK but arguably the most famous is Champneys in Tring, where it all began. A typical itinerary will be:

> You may arrive at the spa from 9.30 am where you will receive a
> short briefing, covering the itinerary of the day. You are then at
> leisure to make the most of the wonderful facilities on offer,
> including the pool, gym, croquet lawn or simply take a relaxing stroll
> around the acres of gardens. You'll each receive a light buffet lunch, a
> La Zouche facial, a La Zouche Massage, manicure and pedicure
> which will leave you feeling relaxed and invigorated. You will receive
> complimentary use of a bathrobe whilst at the Spa.

This particular package is presented through www.buyagift.co.uk or tel: 0870 444 2524. You can also contact Champneys direct on tel: 08703 300 300 or visit www.healthfarms.uk for information on their other health clubs and current prices. Alternatively, for a comprehensive list of what spa treatments and offers are available nationwide tel: 08708 50 55 50 or visit www.spaseekers.com.

SUMMARY

There are so many wonderful experiences available to enjoy that it would take up the entire book if I were to try and cover them all, but I hope the selection above gives you a taster of some of the treats available. Obviously some treats cost more than others, but you do not have to pay the earth to enjoy yourself as there are so many other less costly things to do. You could take a day trip to the seaside with fish and chips and deck chairs, a trip to the cinema, an organised walk, a trip to the theatre or cinema, afternoon tea in the park, a visit to a museum, or a stroll along a county lane to name but a few. Really a special treat is what you make of it, whether it's a having a candle-lit dinner for two in your home . . . or splashing out and eating in a posh restaurant. It's all about having fun and fun does not necessarily have to bust the bank balance . . . ask the kids on the beach with an ice cream and a bucket and spade . . . they know!

9

Working and Retirement

Retirement does not necessarily mean giving up work altogether, even if you do intend to 'Spend The Kids' Inheritance'! You may not be ready to throw in the towel completely, but as you reach a certain age you may want to change your lot, 'work wise', for something new or for a different working practice like part time instead of full time. As jobs have lost their 'cradle to the grave' status, coupled with considerable pension cutbacks it is not such a bad thing to take early retirement or even voluntary redundancy, should the price be right. However, if you want to change your job and are over 50, you may not find it easy and may need to consult recruitment organisations that specialise in more mature workers.

If your main motivation for staying in work is not financial, you could consider some voluntary work, either in your local charity shop, hospice or even overseas for example. There are lots of opportunities for retired people to get involved in satisfying and rewarding voluntary work.

RETIREMENT AGE

If you have reached the normal retirement age that comes with the job description, your employer has no obligation to keep you on. This is subject to change under the new age discrimination rules which come into effect at the end of 2006. If you want to continue working and have to look for another job there are a few agencies listed below that could help, but there are many more.

- In 2000, 'FiftyOn' recognised that the combination of an ageing demographic with ageist practices could deprive UK companies of a huge talent base. It advertises jobs on behalf of employers that value the power of experience, recognise the benefits that an age diverse workforce can bring and welcomes applications from older candidates. For more information, tel: 0207 451 0231 or visit www.fiftyon.co.uk.
- For information on age discrimination and the workplace, contact the Department for Work and Pensions (DWP) Age Positive Team via their website: www.dwp.gov.uk.
- Contact your local employment agency and enquire about the 'Job Seekers Allowance' and ask about finding employment under the 'New Deal 50 Plus Scheme'. For more information tel: 0845 606 2626 or call their helpline on 0845 606 0680.
- The 'Third Age Employment Network' and 'Third Age Challenge' can also offer help and advice. They are a non profit making company committed to addressing age discrimination issues and finding older people work. Contact tel: 020 7843 1590 or visit www.taen.org.uk.

- Executive Stand-By Ltd finds places for executives in industry – both in commerce and voluntary organisations. The upper age limit is 65 years. For further information contact tel: 01244 323600 or visit www.b2bindex.co.uk.
- Wrinklies Direct are a network of twelve recruitment agencies that specialise in finding employment for older people. Tel: 0870 600 1921 for your nearest office or visit www.wrinklies.org.uk.

The government, as part of its age positive scheme, has information on employers who are part of the campaign and who might therefore be particularly appropriate targets for your job search strategy. Contact your local Job Centre for details.

CONSULTANCY WORK

It is not unusual for people of retirement age to stay on with their existing firm in a consultancy capacity. This can be for specific projects, on a seasonal basis or during busy times of the year. Discuss these possibilities with your employer and if there isn't an opportunity available at your existing company, you may be able to find work on a consultancy basis at another company. Consultancy, by definition, is not limited to a single client and you could build up a steady list of assignments, capitalising on your existing skills. There is always demand for those with knowledge of computers, pensions, public relations and many other areas needing skill and experience. Below are several organisations that you could contact to help you:

- The Institute of Management Consultancy (IMC) might be able to assist you if you are looking for consultant firms to contact. Tel: 0207 7566 5220 or visit www.imc.co.uk.
- The Institute of Business Advisers has contacts with business advice centres and enterprise agencies. There is a registration fee and they will only consider applicants with substantial business experience. For further information tel: 01246 453322 or visit www.iba.org.uk.

INTERIM MANAGEMENT

This has been one of the largest growth areas in recruitment in the past few years. The term covers an enormous range of job opportunities which can be due to emergency, supervising closure, or any other temporary assignment, e.g. installing a new computer system or starting up a marketing campaign. There are many companies to choose from including:

- Interim Management Association: 0207 462 3294 or visit www. inteimmanagementuk.com.
- Albermarle Interim Management Services Plc: 0207 079 3737 or visit www.albermarleinterim.com.
- Penna Interim: 0207 663 6887 or www.e-penna.com.
- Executive Management: 01962 829 705 or visit www.Executives online.co.uk.

SECONDMENT

If you are still a couple of years from retirement and you work for a large organisation, there may be secondment opportunities. You could also ask your employer if they would consider sending you on a secondment to do voluntary work, to an enterprise agency, a charity or to help a local small business. The company would need to agree to pay your salary and other benefits. For some large companies, helping other small businesses and charities can be a good marketing ploy, so there is something to be gained for them too. Business in the Community specialises in coordinating secondments. For any further information, contact tel: 0870 600 2482 or www.bitc.org.uk. If you are in Scotland call 0131 442 2020 or visit www.sbcs.com.

MARKET RESEARCH

There are many opportunities in market research, particularly for those with knowledge of market research techniques. The work can involve interviewing people on the street, talking to them on the telephone, preparing questionnaires, collecting data and statistical analysis. Some knowledge of IT skills can be an advantage. For a list of all market research agencies there is *The Research Buyers Guide* which is available from the Market Research Society: tel: 0207 490 4911 or www.mrs. org.uk. There is a fee for this book of approximately £40.

THE NATIONAL CENTRE FOR SOCIAL RESEARCH

No experience is necessary to become a freelance interviewer for the National Centre for Social Research. You may be required to interview people on the street or in their home. These surveys can be on many topics such as education, health or housing. Applicants must have the use of a car and be computer literate. Two days paid training are given to applicants at the start. Contact The National Centre for Research, tel: 0207 250 1866 or visit www.natcen.ac.uk.

SALES

Almost every commercial firm in the land is on the lookout for a salesperson with that extra something . . . so if that is you, then you will probably not need to read this section as you will no doubt be inundated with work opportunities. There is always a demand for people to sell 'advertising space', demonstrate products in shops and basically to sell anything, anywhere! Selling today is not just standing in a shop or chasing sceptical customers. Telesales has caught on in a big way and if selling anything really grabs you, then you could make more money in retirement than ever before. Direct selling is the UK's largest provider of part-time, independent earning opportunities. It is an ideal way to start a business of your own and offers many unique and rewarding opportunities. Direct selling is a method of selling goods directly to the consumer and accounts for total sales in excess of £2 billion every year. It is usually made face-to-face – either where a product is demonstrated in the home or a catalogue is left with the customer. For further information contact the Direct Selling Association on tel: 0207 497 1234 or visit www.dsa.org.uk.

STARTING YOUR OWN BUSINESS

It is an interesting fact that people starting a business in their 50s have twice the survival rate of people setting up a business in their 20s. For any business to be successful, however, it is going to take a lot of work. So if you are not up for it then don't start it! Contact your local Business Link on tel: 0845 600 9006 or www.businesslink.gov.uk. For Business Connect in Wales contact tel: 01792 817575 or visit www.bcnpt.co.uk. For Scottish Enterprise in Scotland call: 0845 607 8787 or visit www.scottish-enterprise.com for helpful information and advice. Some points to consider would be:

- Have you got what it takes to become a successful entrepreneur?
- Are you committed to running a business in retirement and all of the hard work and responsibility it entails?
- Are you willing to learn and adapt to new things?
- Are you willing to sacrifice the 'free time' that retirement offers?
- Are you capable of making decisions on your own and do you have 'people skills'?
- Is your partner supportive and willing to help?
- Can you afford to invest in yourself and do you understand the financial side of running a business?
- Are you ready and enthusiastic for a career change?

Training

Anyone considering starting a business in retirement will need to have some idea of how that business will work. A useful way of gaining work experience is to go and work unpaid for someone else in the same line of business. You should also try and attend as many classes as you can find on subjects such as book keeping, accountancy, computer skills and sales techniques. Also, if you know of someone who is already a success in the business of your choice, do not be afraid to ask their advice. Be certain about what kind of business you want to take on and do as much research into the practicalities as you can. In order to be successful you will need to know about any local competitors, what prices they charge, their reputation and the services they offer. You may also have to be prepared not to earn an income immediately, as it may be some time before your business realises a profit. You will need operating capital; call: 0845 601 5962 or visit www.clearlybusiness.com for free information and order *Starting and Running Your Own Business*. You should also visit www.myownbusiness.org. Below are just a few examples of business ideas that would suit retirees:

- antique dealership
- B&B or running a pub
- property development, buy to let, let to buy
- garden maintenance
- painting and decorating
- catering
- home handy man services
- information services
- domestic cleaning and laundry services
- interior design
- desktop publishing
- floristry
- photography
- opening a shop
- import and export services
- opening a dog grooming salon.

A business plan

You will need to draw up a business plan. In the plan you will need to explain how your business works in practice. You will also need to describe your objectives and where you see your business going. It is important to have a clear view of the marketplace and what your competition is likely to be. You will want to include details of your commercial policy, regarding sales or services and you will need to develop a strategy to market your idea. Other items you will need to cover are your financial position, how much (if any) money you will need to raise and how you plan to repay any loans. It is also important to include how your product differs from the competition and why you think people will choose your services. You will also have to consider what type of trader you want to be:

♦ a sole trader
♦ forming a partnership
♦ forming a limited company.

RUNNING A FRANCHISE

You may have always wanted to start your own business, but have been too afraid to whilst you have had to be the provider. Now that you are semi-retired/retired or have decided on a job change, it's up to you what you do with your time. If you still need to earn money then you could look at taking out a franchise. More than 90% of franchises are still trading profitably after five years and you can have the best of both worlds by running your own business with the professional backup of an established network. Check out www.ukbetheboss.com for advice and comprehensive information on the different types of franchises on offer.

RUNNING A PUB

Running a pub is a full-time job which requires a lot of stamina and hardly fits in with the retirement image. Most 'retirees' opt for the gentler alternative of running a B&B. However, if running a pub still interests you as a career change/retirement option then there are a few points you should consider before 'diving in':

♦ The hours are long and when you are not playing 'the host' you will be busy doing the paperwork.

- There will be all the other 'day-to-day' running issues that you will have to deal with.
- You can buy your own 'Free House' outright but as a tenant you would have to take out a lease and the cost of this will be dependent on the length of lease, location and size.
- As a leaseholder you would be self-employed and responsible for any staff.
- You would be required to enforce licensing laws and fire regulations and any other laws that you come into contact with.
- If you are over 50 then some experience either in the leisure industry or some other form of self-employment will be vital if you are to make a success of running a pub.
- The British Institute of Innkeeping advise that you try running a pub for a six month period, prior to taking on a tenancy, to see if it is for you. For further information on training courses and qualifications tel: 01276 684449 or visit www.bii.org.
- For details of tenancies available and 'Free Houses' look in *The Licensee and Morning Advertiser* and *The Publican*, available from newsagents.

RUNNING A B&B

On the plus side you can play host to interesting visitors from all over the world. It doesn't really matter what age you are, as long as you are in good health and can cope with the work. You will be able to employ cookery and interior design skills and, of course, management responsibilities such as hiring staff and being in control of the finances. A B&B can also provide work for the family, as in Villa Sibillini (see p. 106). You are your own boss and many of the expenses of running your home will be tax deductible. Depending on how many rooms you want to rent out you could enjoy a part-time or a full-time income. If your business is seasonal, you can cater to a ski crowd or summer holiday makers, then travel during the off season.

Getting started

Buying an existing B&B has the advantages of being furnished, having future bookings and having already established a reputation (make sure it's a good one, although word soon gets around about new management). You can also scout around for a property that has potential to be a B&B. Should your home be situated in the right location with the facilities for an easy conversion, you could start a B&B in your own home. You will also need to research applying for licences, permits, insurance and any other costs involved with the day-to-day running of a B&B, e.g. food handling, heating and maintenance.

Setting room rates

If you are unsure about room rates check with your local tourist information centre to find out what the going rate is. If your rooms differ greatly in size, facilities and outlook this will have to be reflected in your price and some rooms will generate more income than others, particularly if they have a view or en-suite facilities (a must these days).

Taking reservations

You will need to have a strategy for taking bookings and this is covered in the Retirement Homes and Holiday Lets chapter. You will also need to compile a guest registration form. Other areas you will need to consider are:

◆ cancellation policy
◆ B&B house rules, such as breakfast times and whether to accept pets
◆ dietary requirements
◆ guests safety
◆ the fire exit strategy which should be clearly displayed in all rooms
◆ what to include in a continental breakfast or full breakfast
◆ other food you might choose to offer
◆ housekeeping check lists.

Marketing your B&B

Marketing your B&B will be the most important way to kick start and maintain your business. There are several ways of doing this and you could employ an agency to advertise your B&B and take care of all the reservation issues, including cancellations. They will take a percentage of your rates for this service. You can also:

◆ Create a website. Hire an expert web page designer to ensure you get a professional job. Don't try to do this yourself unless you really know what you are doing. The more professional a website is, the more custom it is likely to attract.

◆ Promote your B&B in directories.

◆ Market your B&B to people with special interests.

◆ Fill the B&B off season, with other possibilities for generating income such as weddings, romantic weekends, business seminars and other specialised events.

Repeat business

The most important aspect to running a B&B is getting repeat business. Therefore, it is important that you try to stay in touch with your guests and keep them updated with any special offers or events you might be hosting. You will also need to keep up to date with what the competition is doing or what new regulations are applicable, all of which you can do by attending seminars and conferences for B&B owners.

Suppliers

You will need to source suppliers for the best and freshest produce available. 'Farm fresh eggs' carry a little more interest then just 'eggs', as does 'home cured bacon' or 'freshly grown tomatoes' all of which tend to be much tastier than the supermarket brands. You will also need to source:

- cleaning products for the hotel industry
- coffee makers
- bedding, hypo allergenic bedding and towels
- soaps and shampoos
- chocolates to place on pillows (if you want to add that special touch).

Satisfaction

Running a B&B will be hard work, but it could be very rewarding. You cannot satisfy all of the people, all of the time. But if your standards are high you will get pleasure out of pleasing most of the people, most of the time. Getting that all important repeat business, building a good reputation and, above all, making some money for yourself and your family.

BUY TO LET

The principle of 'buy to let' is that the investor purchases the property in order to enjoy long term capital gains whilst the tenant pays the mortgage. Alternatively if your aim is to generate an income from your investment, choose properties for their suitability to deliver good rental yields rather than for their potential to deliver a profit from short term house price rises.

Yield

The yield is the percentage of what you earn from renting out your 'buy to let' property, after all the expenses of purchasing and the running costs are subtracted. An example of a gross yield, before property deductions, such as voids, ground rent, service charge, fees and property outgoings would be:

- £100.000 purchases an apartment.
- A 10% rental income would be £10,000.
- This would represent a 10% (gross) yield.

What is considered a good net yield?

A good net yield can range from 7% to 10%. This is not always possible to achieve and depends on the area you invest in. If the local market is saturated with similar flats, this will have a negative effect on your anticipated yield. There will be a lot of competition to get tenants as supply will outweigh demand. Rents will be reduced and standards will have to be high if you are to avoid voids.

Expenses

Make a list of all the expenses (including mortgage and other property related costs) you anticipate will occur before you invest. If the profit margins are too tight and the rental does not net you enough income, then it is likely that this property will not be the right investment for you . . . if your main objective is yield.

What type of property should I choose?

A general rule of thumb is that apartments are the preferred rental properties in inner city areas, whereas houses are more suitable in small towns and rural locations. If you are in any doubt at all as to what property will be most suitable for letting in a given area, consult the professionals and read the local property papers.

Investing in 'buy to let' for capital growth

This is where you invest in a property where the anticipated yield of that property will not cover the mortgage or net you any income. In fact the property could be termed a liability rather than an asset because it actually costs you money to rent it out. This situation is common in inner city areas where markets are saturated.

What are the advantages of buying a property like this?

If you are buying a property that is costing you money to run it will be because you believe that property will increase in value enough to cover losses and net you a handsome profit when you choose to sell it. There is no reason to suspect that this will not happen in a rising market. If the market falls however, you could end up in a negative equity situation where the property costs you more than it is worth when you choose to sell it. Obviously if the market is falling, it is better to hang onto the property if you can, rather than sell in a falling market. This will be entirely dependent on your own personal circumstances.

Let to buy

This can be another way of making money in retirement. It is the reverse of 'buy to let' and instead of selling your own house when you move, you re-mortgage, refurbish and then rent it out. This way you own two homes; one which you are living in, the other which you are renting out, ideally for enough money to cover your mortgage and net you an income. It also means that when you come to sell either property you will be entitled to tapered capital gains relief, depending on how long you have lived in each property.

Teaching/home tutors

If you have been teaching full-time and want to continue to work in that area in retirement, then you are well placed, as home tutors are always in demand. If you are good at what you do, word soon spreads amongst parents and you could find that you have more work than you can cope with. There are several agencies that can help you find work such as:

- Tel: 0208 854 8024 or visit www.exceltutors.co.uk.
- Tel: 0870 7607 451 or visit www.agewiserecruitment.co.uk.
- Tel: 0870 774 8811 or visit www.jobsite.co.uk.
- Tel: 0845 847 6199 or visit www.executivejobhunters.co.uk.

Home sitters

This means taking care of someone's home whilst they are away. You may also be required to look after their pets. You will get paid for this depending upon the size of the house and responsibilities involved. Food and travel are also included and if the house is pleasantly located it could be like a paid holiday. Alternatively you can look after someone's pet in your own home or offer your services as a dog walker if you enjoy being outdoors. Companies specialising in this type of work are:

- Tel: 01296 630730 or www.homesitters.co.uk.
- Tel: 0800 013 0026 or www.guardianangelsservices.co.uk.
- Tel: 020 7738 8937 or www.universalaunts.co.uk.

Nursing

Qualified nurses are always in demand all over the country and are likely to find work through their local hospital or, alternatively, through a nursing agency. If you are not qualified and are interested in becoming a care attendant, you can apply to work for the charity Crossroads on tel: 0845 4500350 or visit www.crossroads.org.uk, which provides temporary relief for carers of sick or disabled people in their own homes.

Childminding

If you are active and enjoy looking after the grandchildren, you could consider childminding, be it for one child or more, depending on how much work you want to take on. For further information about registering as a childminder contact your local social services department.

Cooking

If you enjoy cooking and have a flair for it, this could be a way of making money in retirement, ranging in scale from selling jam to having your own label for specialised chutneys. You could also cater for other people's dinner parties. Start with friends and family at first, until you find your feet and find out whether it suits you and is financially viable. Then you can begin to advertise your services in the local newspaper or through a catering agency. Before you advertise think about whether you are committed to maximising your opportunities and can handle all the problems an expanding business may bring. Tel: 0117 330 8910 or visit www.duport.co.uk for general information on how to set up a company.

DIY

If you are a 'bit handy' around the house then there are always people out there who need a job doing. Contact your local Age Concern and offer your services as a handyman. Doing jobs for friends and family can help provide you with a reputation for good work and reliability if you are skilled. If you are good, you will soon be able to take on as much or as little work you want. See Chapter 4, Hobbies and Learning.

Gardening

This may have been your favourite hobby. If you enjoy it and are creative and knowledgeable, you could help people with their gardens. Looking after one person's garden will soon generate other business. This could range from simple garden maintenance, such as cutting lawns, to the more ambitious landscape gardening and design, but this is dependent on your skills. See Chapter 4, Hobbies and Learning.

Dress making and soft furnishings

We have all probably come across a 'nimble fingers' in our time making amongst other things, bridesmaid dresses, cushions and curtains. If you have dress making skills and enjoy it, you could consider setting up an alteration and dressmaking business or a soft furnishing business. Again, you will get most of your initial work from friends and family, but your contacts will grow as people learn about your skills. So, if you enjoy working and sourcing fabric, why not try making a few soft furnishing items such as cushions and throws. Try taking on a market stall to see how well your merchandise sells. If it goes well, you could have the beginnings of a successful business. There will be courses available through your local education department. See Chapter 4, Hobbies and Learning.

Charity/voluntary work

www.mobi.co.uk is a non-profit making public charity whose aim is to provide free educational coursework to foster successful entrepreneurs via the Internet. You would have to commit to reading through the entire course before you started and be available to volunteer from 8 hours to 40 hours a week. A minimum schedule commitment of three months would be required.

Voluntary Service Overseas (VSO)

VSO is an international development charity that works through volunteers.

Its aim is to bring people together to share skills, creativity and learning to build a fairer world. The organization welcomes volunteers from an ever increasing range of countries, backgrounds and ages. National agencies in Canada, Kenya, the Netherlands, the Philippines and India recruit volunteers from many different countries worldwide. The idea being, that instead of sending food or money, they send men and women, people from all different professions who want to make a difference in the fight against poverty. These volunteers work in partnership with colleagues and communities to share skills, learning and jointly achieve change. VSO are realistic in their expectations, commit to long-term development goals and long-term partnerships rather than offer short-term solutions. VSO is by far the largest independent volunteer-sending agency in the world. Since 1958, they claim to have sent out more than 29,000 volunteers to work in Africa, Asia, and the Caribbean, the Pacific region and, more latterly, Eastern Europe.

What skills do volunteers need?

The skills needed are varied, as the communities you would be helping are 'developing':

- You would be required to use your professional skills to train and advise colleagues in your area of expertise.
- You would live and work within the local community, usually for two years. You must be able to work creatively and adapt to unfamiliar situations – often with few resources.

To enable you to take on this challenge you'll get:

- A living allowance, accommodation, insurance, flights, individually tailored training, support and advice pre-departure.
- Networking opportunities with other volunteers, grants and advice to help you settle in on your return to your home country.

Tel: 0208 780 7200 or visit www.vso.org.uk for further information.

SUMMARY

You may think that working in retirement is the last thing that you want to do and if that is how you feel . . . good luck to you! You may have to work in retirement due to financial needs or dwindling pensions and it should be possible to do that with the help of the suggestions above.

You may want to work for other reasons not necessarily financial, such as charity work. This would enable you to give something back in retirement and do something for others and enjoy the challenge and satisfaction that would bring. Particularly if it involves doing something that you have always wanted to do but never had the time. Whatever you decide . . . the great thing about retirement . . . is that it is your choice . . . it's up to you what you choose to do.

10

Building Your Dream Retirement Home

Retired people decide to build their own homes for all sorts of reasons (apart from 'Spending The Kids' Inheritance') such as being able to choose where they want to live right down to the plot of land they want to build on. They can design the whole layout and specification of their house, so it is tailor made to their needs. It costs less (assuming it has come in on budget) as most self-build homes work out at 20% to 30% cheaper than if you purchased a new house on the same plot. There can be a sense of satisfaction that you have been part of creating something you truly want, at a time of your life when compromise shouldn't be an issue. These are some of the more positive aspects of building your own home. The downside, of course, is that even doing the smallest building job is not without problems from dodgy builders, incomplete deliveries, weather, absenteeism, late deliveries, mistakes, companies going into liquidation and lost orders. In fact, the list is endless. The most important thing to remember is that very few estimated completion dates are accurate as most building programmes incur some delay, somewhere along the line. So, to start a self-building project, thinking that everything will be plain sailing would be foolish. Expect the worst and you'll be surprised when it doesn't turn out as bad as you predicted. The result will be worth it in the end as long as you try to stay within budget and in control!

THE EASY WAY – THE KIT HOME

There are literally thousands of companies offering Modular Kit homes. Prefabricated, manufactured in a factory, delivered in kit form to your building plot and quickly assembled, either by your own builder or the company that supplies it. It is possible to choose from a whole range of types and styles of housing, with designs literally 'off the peg', ranging from the modernistic German 'Huf Haus' to a more traditional 'green oak' framed house, a North American style home, a Finnish log cabin, a modest bungalow or a 'heritage' style home. If you want to design your own house, with or without an architect, that is no problem either. What is exciting about this type of building is that because so much of the 'build' happens in a regulated factory environment, it will be more efficient, quicker and less stressful than a more traditional build. Most of these designs also incorporate a lot of new technology which makes them incredibly energy efficient and environmentally friendly. From an investment point of view a kit home, when properly installed and maintained, will appreciate in the same way as the surrounding 'site-built' homes. Just to get a taste of how many companies are operating in this market visit www.selfbuildabc.co.uk.

Where do I find a plot?

The first thing that you will need is a plot with planning permission to build on. You will have to do a great deal of research but try the following:

- The local papers often advertise land for sale.
- Auctions often sell plots of land, so it is worth investigating a few to find out what is on offer.
- Estate agents.
- Planning applications (check local papers).
- Building plot and land databases on the Internet.
- Check out your local area. Look out for any waste-land or dis-used/derelict buildings. If you see anything you are interested in, contact your local planning office to find out what the situation is.
- Get a detailed map and thoroughly explore the area of your choice.

Remember, you will have an overall budget to consider and you have a house to build, so don't spend more than you can afford on the plot.

Choosing an architect

This will be one of the most important elements of your self-build project. The things to look out for when making a decision are:

- Creative skills, imagination and flair (no amount of qualifications will be able to compensate for these if they don't come naturally).
- The ability to listen to what the client wants and not blind them with science and unnecessary technical talk.
- Do you like them? (This will be very important as you will be working together a lot.)
- Track record. All reputable architects should be proud of their work and will be only too happy to show and discuss their portfolio with you.

- Real experience of designing an individual home, as opposed to a large development or commercial project.
- Awareness of current building costs.
- A willingness to discuss fees.
- An understanding of your specific budget requirements and limitations.

The clients contribution

It is important that you are clear about what you want. Where possible take photographs of houses that you like. Cut out any pictures of properties that interest you from newspapers and magazines. If you want to have a go at drawing a rough plan yourself then do so, at least this will give the architect/designer an idea of what you are after, even if you are not Michelangelo!

Clarity

Be very clear from the outset about your budget and stipulate that the construction costs must not exceed that figure, as there is no pot of gold hidden under the floorboards. Explain that your ceiling price is your final price and that you have no margin for extras.

Be in control

During the construction process you may have to compromise on your original design for financial or practical reasons. Be flexible about these issues but if you are not happy about any changes, do not be rushed into any decisions. Take time to explore whether there are other ways to get what you want and, if not, be prepared to compromise . . . but only compromise if you are sure that you can be happy with it . . . after all it's your dream home.

Personal recommendation

If you know someone who recently has had some work done on their house which you like, and which has involved the services of an architect then ask them if they would recommend their architect. If all has gone to plan and they are pleased with the outcome, they will be happy to do this. If it has been trouble all the way, even if the end result looks good, you may want to look elsewhere, as a stressed working relationship may not be the best option. It is important to remember, however, that as with all business relationships where personalities are involved, you need to make your own decision.

The local planning office

Although they will not be able to directly recommend architects, they will be able to give you a list of names that they have worked with in the past and it should not take Sherlock Holmes to work out which ones they prefer. Alternatively, if there is a recently built property that you admire you can always ask the planning office to see the drawings relating to that site and they will have the name of the architect on them. This will also be a good way of assessing how the plan was presented to the council and ascertaining how the plans were received by them.

Trade associations

As with all trade associations just because they are listed doesn't mean that they are the best. But if you have no other way of sourcing a good architect then they are certainly a place to start from. You can get a list of architects in your area from:

◆ The Royal Institute of British Architects Advisery Service: 0207 580 5533 or visit www.riba.org.
◆ Associated Self-build Architects: 0800 387 310 or visit www.asba-architects.org.
◆ The Architects Registration Board: 0207 278 2206 or visit www.arb.org.uk.
◆ The British Institute of Architectural Technologists: 0207 278 2206 or visit www.biat.org.uk.

The local papers

Some companies advertise in the local press as to what type of architectural services they offer.

UNDERSTANDING GOOD DESIGN PRINCIPLES

Whether you choose to employ an architect or not, it is important that you understand good basic design principles. You may, in retirement want to do some work from home and even if you don't . . . from a re-sale point of view it would be advisable to consider providing 'a work space' in your overall design. It is also important that you provide at least two bathrooms, as this is an essential for modern day living. Other aspects which add value are large rooms, natural light and spacious kitchens. Not only will good design principles help you create your ideal home, they will also make sound investment sense.

FIRST FINANCIAL STEPS

You will need to finance your self-build property and must have a mortgage agreed in principle even if you are 'Spending the Kids' Inheritance'. There are specialist lenders that offer mortgages for home-building projects. You will need to refer to the individual lender for details of their stage payment system in their terms and conditions. Most mortgage companies will release stage payments in arrears so it is important to ascertain what your financial requirements will be during the construction phases. A few mortgage companies will release stage payments in advance. The mortgage can be anything from 75% to 95% of the building costs and 75% to 95% of the land costs. You will need to have some form of planning consent before the mortgage company will release funds on the land.

Sufficient funds initially

You need to ensure that you have sufficient funds during the initial construction period and sufficient cash flow to fund the project between each stage payment. If you are doubtful about your cash flow and have no short-term savings to fall back on, you should consider a self-build mortgage that offers advance stage payments, but even with this there could still be a gap between each payment.

Using equity in your own home

Most retirees choose to raise money by using equity from their own home, in conjunction with a mortgage, which makes stage payments, from a bank or building society. This could mean that your stage payments would be coupled with the existing payments on your home loan, enabling you to stay in your current home until your new property is built.

Deposit

As with most mortgage offers you will have to come up with a deposit and this can be from the sale of your own home, the equity raised on your home or from savings.

Reclaiming VAT on a new build

If you are constructing a new building, the good news is that you can reclaim the VAT on most materials purchased for the house build. The bad news is that you cannot claim this VAT back until the house is finished. Contact your local VAT Business Advice Office (see your local telephone directory) for a claim form and information leaflets.

The budget

This will be dependent on many factors which you will need to decide on before any construction begins. You will have to consider how big you want your property to be. How many storeys it will have, the internal layout and how much of the building project you intend to involve yourself in, as this will have an affect on the overall labour costs. As foundations and roof work are two of the most expensive elements in any build, a bungalow will work out almost as expensive as a two storey house on the same external ground area.

YOUR INVOLVEMENT IN THE CONSTRUCTION

If you choose to project manage the build yourself and you have the time and the knowledge, this will obviously work out cheaper than employing a project manager. It will be your job to make sure that all materials are delivered on time and that the correct contractors and labour are able to get on with their jobs at the allotted time. This is not easy and, if you want a stress free retirement, not advisable as even with professionals on board it will be quite stressful enough!

The project manager/main contractor

If you are new to the self-build game and unless you know a considerable amount about building work, you would be advised to employ someone to project manage the development for you. This could be the architect who has drawn up the plans. He or she will already have been in consultation with you and the local planning office to get the plans approved and, if necessary, modified. It could also be a builder who has knowledge of the local workforce and has a track record of similar projects undertaken before.

Builders

It will be the project manager's job to deal with the builders and it will also be their responsibility to order the materials and to make sure that they are delivered on site at the required time. The project manager will also ensure that the building programme runs to schedule which will involve the orchestration of electricians, plumbers, carpenters and anyone else connected with the build. Their other and most important burden will be to control the budget!

How do I find a good project manager?

A good builder may not necessarily be a good project manager. If you are considering using a builder, check whether they have done any other similar projects in the past and ask to see their work if possible. If not, ask for references from previously satisfied clients and ask whether you can speak to them personally to check on the 'job satisfaction' level. If the builder has lots of unfinished projects on the go, then be aware that you could end up being one of those unfinished projects. If the builder's last job has fallen significantly behind schedule or has encountered other problems, he may not want you to see it and, if he doesn't, take that as a warning sign.

Personality clash

Do not employ someone as your project manager whom you suspect you will not get along with. It is important to have a good relationship with your project manager, as this relationship will most likely be put to the test at some point during the building programme. Sometimes a clash of personalities can put the project at risk as much, if not more so, than an unreliable workforce.

Personal recommendation

If you know a good builder, plumber or electrician then they most likely will know other professionals whom they are prepared to recommend. It is possible to source most of your workforce from one skilled professional. If they employ good working practices, it is more than likely that the people they recommend will employ the same high standards too.

DIY project managing

If you are project managing the development yourself then you will need to have a lot of organisational skills in getting the building programme to run smoothly. You will also need a good plumber, electrician and plasterer as well as a builder. In fact, I would have an army of them standing by!

Software

If you are going it alone, check out what software is available to help you plan your budget strategy. Some can estimate the cost of your building project and manage the process from start to finish. These include new builds, extensions, renovations and conversions, from either a small plan or a full working drawing.

Suppliers

It will also be important for you to get a good supplier, where you can order your building materials at trade prices. If you are employing a main contractor they will have their own preferred suppliers and will already have a trade account in place.

THE COST OF MATERIALS

This will depend on what type of finish you are trying to achieve.

◆ If you are going for standard materials, this will comply with specification levels provided by most house builders. It will be more off the peg, than custom built.

◆ If you are going for a better finish, this will cost more but you will get a superior kitchen, joinery, insulation, quality sanitary ware, under-floor heating.

◆ If you are going for a top of the range finish, with bespoke kitchen, high performance insulation, under-floor heating, hardwood joinery and designer bathrooms then expect to pay top of the range prices.

Quality building materials survey

If you are planning the build using stone, natural slate, thatch, handmade bricks, flint panels, timber or more ecologically friendly materials, you will have to do the budget with these extra costs in mind, as they will be considerably more expensive than standard materials.

Ground conditions

The ground conditions need to be tested by an engineer as soon as possible. You will not be able to do a comprehensive budget until the site ground conditions have been assessed. If the ground is sloping, or the site has unusual ground conditions, such as clay or any kind of contamination, this can substantially add to your building costs.

Where should I live during the build?

If you are retired, you will need to think very carefully about this, as the build may take a considerable time. You may consider yourself too old to be living out of a suitcase, on other people's floors or even throwing yourself at the mercy of relatives. The ideal would be to stay in your present home as long as possible, but if you have had to sell your home and release the capital to fund the deposit then you will need somewhere to live. You will have to budget into your overall expenditure the cost of a mobile home (not ideal) or rented accommodation, which would be preferable. You will also have to factor into your budget any costs related to storing your furniture.

INSURANCE

Insurance is an essential part of any self-build programme. You will not only have to insure your property against damage and theft, you will also have to insure it against personal injury. This means that anyone working on, or visiting your development is covered, should there be an accident. The insurance cover can also include any mobile home situated on the site. The insurance should cover:

- Public liability insurance.
- Employers liability insurance.
- Contract works insurance.
- Building warranty: NHBC or ZURICH.

Other additional costs

There will be many other costs involved with any self-build project and it is important that these are all calculated into your budget. If you are in doubt about a price, overestimate rather than underestimate. It is always preferable to have money left over, rather than be caught out because of insufficient funds. Other costs will include:

- land costs
- legal fees/stamp duty/land tax
- topographical survey fees
- mortgage fees
- design fees
- planning application/building regulations fees
- structural guarantee/insurance
- connection of services such as water, electricity, gas and drainage
- demolition works if applicable
- landscaping.

PLANNING PERMISSION

It is good to get this ball rolling as soon as possible, as this can often take a frustratingly long time to get. It is always advisable to employ a professional who is well versed with the peculiarities of the planning department to guide you through this process and fill in all the necessary applications. This can be a designer, architect or a planning consultant.

BUILDING REGULATIONS

This will involve sending in an application form with detailed drawings showing the site location, service locations and block plan. You will then be allocated a Building Control Surveyor who will look at your plans in detail. If your application conforms to building regulations you will be issued an approval notice.

What if my building application is refused?

The reasons for the refusal will be documented and you will be allowed to amend these and re-submit the plans again without further expense.

If the plans are still refused and you think this is unjustified you will need to seek dispensation from the local council and if that fails you will have to apply to the Department of the Secretary of State. Your Building Control Surveyor will be able to provide you with the details if you choose this course of action.

Before starting any work on site
Make sure that you contact the necessary authorities in connection with providing temporary services, such as water and power. If you are employing a project manager, arranging these services will be part of his job.

Expensive design options
If you want to 'Spend The Kids' Inheritance' then you could go for the more bespoke, luxurious options such as:

+ complex shapes
+ top of the range kitchen
+ home cinema
+ bespoke fittings
+ jacuzzi/sauna/hot tub.

SUMMARY
Self-build is becoming increasingly popular with 10% of all new houses built each year by self-builders. The most crucial aspect of any self-build project is not only the planning, but also to get the right people in place at the right time. If you are retired you may have the time to organise this but you should not underestimate the skill involved in scheduling building works. You will also need to shop around for your supplier and constantly check that the materials on order are to be delivered on time. This could put a spanner into your building works if you have tradespeople booked in who are not able to get on with their job on

the day. If you do employ good tradespeople (and hopefully you will) then look after them. Make the experience a positive one for the entire workforce. Stay in control and constantly plan and re-plan and if the jigsaw just does not fit . . . don't be afraid to call in a professional!

11

Property Development in Retirement

Maybe you are a bit of a DIY enthusiast whose retirement dream has always been to keep active and go into some form of property development be it to sell on, rent out or live in. Property development can be very stressful, so it is not for the faint hearted, but if it is a challenge you are looking for in retirement and you are fit enough, then property development could be for you. You will need the help of good professionals, especially a builder, and once you have found one that you can trust, you will need to treat them well as reliable builders are hard to find. It is important to enjoy a good relationship with your builder as it will help make the building programme run much smoother.

SURVEYS

Before you commit to purchasing any type of property for renovation you will need to have a survey done. You will not be able to get a mortgage offer without one and if you are buying the property outright you will still need a survey to evaluate what works are necessary. There are three types of survey:

- A basic valuation: this will look at the structure of the house and any other issues that could affect the properties value. The surveyor will also value the property and the building society or bank will offer you a mortgage based upon that valuation. The cost of the valuation report will depend on the size and value of the house.
- A Homebuyers Survey: this can be done at the same time as the basic valuation and will work out cheaper if they both are done together. A Homebuyers Survey is more detailed than the basic valuation. It will look at the general décor of the property, as well as looking for any defects. It is not foolproof, however, as surveyors tend to survey only what they can see. They will not lift carpets, look under floorboards or scramble around on roofs.
- A full structural survey: this is a comprehensive survey that is done by a fully qualified chartered surveyor. It is generally only necessary for properties that are in any way unusual or older properties where there may be a considerable amount of refurbishment to be done. This detailed survey is for the benefit of the borrower only, and will be quite expensive as the surveyor will have to write you a fully comprehensive report. Specialist help may be recommended by the surveyor.

PLANNING CONSENTS

If you are considering refurbishing a property then you may need to obtain planning consents before you purchase the property or before any work can be undertaken.

Planning permission

If you are replacing 'like with like', e.g. a new conservatory which is equal in size, then planning permission needn't be sought. If you are considering building an extension that is in excess of 50 cubic feet, you may well need planning permission. If you build anything without planning permission, you could be served with an Enforcement Order from the Local Planning Office. They will make you take it down or force you to rebuild it within existing planning consents. If you build an extension, or anything similar, without planning permission, you could have a problem selling the property, as the buyer's solicitor will want to see copies of planning consents.

Conservation areas

If the home you want to renovate is in a conservation area you will need planning consent before you can alter anything externally. The aim of a conservation area is to 'conserve' anything that could be considered of architectural significance. Conservationists will differ in their opinions as to what is allowed and what isn't, as there are no hard and fast rules. Whether they will be sympathetic to your requests or not, could just be a matter of which side of bed they got out on that day!

BUILDING REGULATIONS

There are two levels of Building Regulation Requirements. Both applications are obtainable from you Local Planning Office:

♦ The building notice: this is only required for minor works and will involve a site visit by the building inspector to check that the correct regulations are being followed.
♦ A full plans application: this will involve sending copies of the working plan to the building inspector for his approval.

If the property is leasehold, check that the freeholder will grant permission before you undertake any changes. Also check whether there are any restrictions in the lease, regarding any alterations you may wish to make to the property, before you purchase.

Vat on conversions

If you are converting an existing property you can claim for materials and also for the services of a plumber, electrician or any other specialist service provider. VAT registered builders must charge the reduced VAT rate of 9% on labour and materials as you will be able to claim this back after the property is complete. Details are outlined in the leaflet entitled *VAT Refunds for 'do-it-yourself builders and converters'* which is available from your local VAT office.

RETIRING, RENOVATING AND LIVING IN THE PROPERTY

If you are planning to retire and live in the property, you may not want to, or be able to afford to (dependent on the extent of the refurbishment), do the renovation work all at once. As you won't be doing the renovation for immediate profit, this shouldn't be a problem. Nor should the timescale, as it will be directly governed by you as to what gets done when, and in which order of priority. If your property needs a total renovation and is for the most part uninhabitable, you may not want to live in the property whilst the work takes place, so this could be an expense that you may need to consider in your budget. If you have to live in the house, you will need to get certain rooms done in order to make life easier for yourself. The most important room to get in place will be the kitchen as this is the beating heart of most households and you will, of course, need to have a functioning bathroom! If it is financially and practically possible for you to stay in your present home until the work is complete then that is your best option.

If you are renovating to sell on

If you are renovating the property for a quick turnaround profit, your budget will be tighter, as you will have to pay for all the work to be done in double quick time. The sooner the property is complete, the sooner you will be able to market and sell it, so that the mortgage repayments don't cut into your profit too much. Any mortgage repayments need to be included in the budget for renovation, as do legal costs and stamp duty. Whatever costs you incur, will come out of your anticipated profit, so it is advisable to keep costs low when doing a 'sell on' renovation. The properties that are best for renovation are at the lower to middle range of the market, as these will not require expensive high tech appliances.

If you are renovating to sell on to the higher end of the market

If you are renovating a property to appeal to the higher end of the market, this will make your initial outlay that much greater. You will have to think about state of the art kitchens, granite or stainless steel work surfaces, limestone bathrooms, marble tiles, real wood floors, high quality appliances and energy efficient heating systems, to name but a few. These things do not come cheap and will increase the amount you have to borrow in order to complete the works. This in turn, will increase the mortgage interest that you will have to pay out until the property is sold.

Don't be over ambitious

If you are thinking of renovating a property for re-sale don't be over ambitious with your first property. Aim for a small family house or apartment. It is possible to make a property look good (as long as it is structurally sound) with flair and imagination. You do not need to throw buckets of money at it to achieve a designer touch.

If you are choosing to rent out your property after renovation

This will affect your budget choices. You will not want to put in high specification appliances and fancy finishes. Instead, the renovation should be based on practical and durable lines, with furniture and décor that can stand up to wear and tear. Also, if you are going to rent out a property with a garden, make the garden as low maintenance as possible. Tenants are unlikely to nurture gardens and water plants regularly. If the garden has a lawn, you may want to consider paving it or adding gravel.

CONSERVATORIES

Conservatories are very fashionable and can add value to a property, as they create extra space. A well designed conservatory can enhance the rear of a property. I have seen some stunning conservatories which have been incorporated into the family kitchen and made into an integral part of the house.

Under floor heating

If you are thinking about putting in a conservatory or replacing an existing one, consider installing under floor heating. This works well in conservatories and affords more wall space, as most of the conservatory will be made out of glass where it will be difficult to place a radiator.

When choosing a conservatory company do thorough research!

Some companies go bankrupt and then immediately set up in a different name. So if the company you are thinking of using has no track record, be cautious as you don't want to 'Spend The Kids' Inheritance' lining the pockets of a dodgy conservatory company (of which there are many). Make sure the conservatory company that you are considering placing your order with has a good reputation. Ask to speak to other clients. Don't necessarily go for the cheaper quote and don't sign on the dotted line until you have had time to consider the deal. Remember some conservatory salesmen are very good at the hard sell. When they come to measure up, they can take a long time which can be a ploy to make you feel guilty if you don't place an order with them. If you do sign a contract, make sure you study the terms and conditions thoroughly as these should include a 'seven day cooling off period', should you choose to cancel your order within that time.

LOFT CONVERSIONS

Loft conversions are another great way of adding space and increasing the value of a house. The same principles apply when choosing a loft conversion company as with a conservatory company ... do your research. Most loft companies heavily advertise their work during construction by placing building signs outside the house (at the discretion of the owner). Check with the owners if they are happy with the way the work is progressing and that the project is running to schedule. Make sure you get at least three quotes and insist on references from other satisfied customers. Ask to personally speak to other clients, as written references can be faked, but verbal references are less likely to be so.

Companies House

If a company is Limited then it must be registered with Companies House. You can ask for information regarding the company, which they will provide for a small fee. This information will tell you how long the company has been operating and who the directors are. If the company has only just registered, it may be because they are genuinely starting out, or it may be a warning sign that they have had to change their company name. If you have any doubts about the validity of a company then don't go with them! For more information tel: 0870 33 33 636 or visit www.companieshouse.gov.uk.

BASEMENT CONVERSIONS

It is becoming increasingly popular to convert basements into living spaces. This is because it is often a cheaper route than moving house and has the advantages of increasing the value of the property. In planning terms, a basement is treated as an extension. So if it exceeds 40 cubic metres, you will need to apply for planning permission. In most cases this shouldn't be refused, as basements have little or no visual impact.

Conservation areas/greenbelt

The local policy regarding planning applications for basements will vary from council to council in conservation and green belt areas where planning regulations are tighter. The size of extensions is restricted in these areas and the planning permission granted will affect any future, above ground extension allowances. If you are planning to convert the basement and extend, you may have to compromise on space, as both basement and extension will eat into the 40 cubic metre allowance.

Will it be cost effective?

It will be more expensive than an extension, but the conversion could increase the value of your house by 20% to 30%, so you should be able to recover your costs well when you choose to sell.

Won't it have damp problems?

You will need to have the basement waterproofed and your choice of waterproof system should be dictated by the level of the water table in your area, the type of soil and the foundation type. To assess ground water conditions, you will need to hire a competent structural engineer or someone recommended by the British Structural Waterproofing Association. For further information tel: 0208 866 8339 or visit www.bswa.co.uk.

Won't it be dark?

You will need to construct a light well, which could mean the excavation of all or part of the front garden. You will need planning permission for this which is likely to stipulate that the changes necessary to the front part of the house have little impact on the character and appearance of the property. From the rear, however, there will be more flexibility and it may be possible to incorporate your basement design into the overall look of your garden.

What fire precautions will I need to take?

A fire exit, either through a window or a door must be provided. If it is through a window, the size and position of the window must be within fire regulation conditions.

Will my builder be able to do the work?

Basements require specialist knowledge and it would be prudent to seek a professional company whose expertise is in converting basements. This may be more expensive in the short term, but could save you money on costly repairs in the long term. Basement problems are not instantly apparent and could take a year or so to surface. The NHBC are leaning towards recommending that all basements should be installed and designed by a specialist company.

Recommending builders

Be careful when recommending builders. What works for you, may not work for your friends. Builders don't like losing work, so they will say yes to an agreed timeframe, as opposed to no. You need realistic start dates and realistic completion dates. Always hold a substantial payment back until final completion. Make sure you are happy with the building work before you make payment.

Plumbers

Just because a plumber is Corgi registered doesn't mean that you are necessarily protected as generally you are only covered if they deal with your boiler. If you don't know a good plumber, see if the local tile shop can recommend anyone. They may know of one because they provide tiles for bathrooms and a lot of plumbers prefer to do their own tiling work. Alternatively ask in a bathroom showroom. They may have plumbers that they use regularly with a successful track record. They may not want to pass on their valuable and time pressed plumber's details to you though, so ask nicely.

SUMMARY

If you want a stress free retirement, property development may not be for you as there are always difficult moments during a building programme. This is inevitable, as your life, to a certain extent, gets turned upside down. However, it can be incredibly satisfying, as you really can transform a house and breathe new life into it with a few well made decisions. It will depend how far you want to go with your development, and how many additions you wish to add. Most importantly, from a property developer's point of view, what will be most cost effective. Study other houses in the area to see what home improvements they have done and check what is popular as this can help you achieve maximum profit potential.

12

Taking up a Sport

Retirement is the perfect opportunity to take up a sport, as you will have time on your hands. You will be able to take advantage of being able to book sessions out of peak hours. It will also be an opportunity for keeping yourself fit and active whilst making new friends. Taking up a sport does not have to mean 'Spending The Kids' Inheritance' as it will be dependent on what you choose to do. Swimming in your local pool, for example, will not be expensive, whereas a golfing holiday in Marbella will be. There are many sports to choose from and this choice will be dependent on your own level of physical fitness. To find out what is available in your local area contact The Central Council of Physical Recreation, tel: 0207 854 8500 or visit www.ccpr.org.uk. They represent the interests of the sporting public and they estimate that 29 million people regularly take part in sport or some form of physical recreation, from rugby to country dancing to motor racing and rambling. All these activities are administered and promoted by a governing or representative body. It is these bodies who make up membership of the CCPR who represent:

♦ 270 national governing and representative bodies of sport and recreation.
♦ 150,000 voluntary sports clubs.
♦ Millions of individuals who participate in sport and recreation.

This would be a very long chapter if I were to list all of the sports that are available in the UK, so I have chosen to highlight a few that are popular in retirement.

GOLF

Golf for some is a way of life. It provides fun, excitement and friendship. It is currently enjoyed by approximately four million people across Great Britain and Ireland. Golf is big business particularly with Northern Europeans who cannot get enough of the game! Golfing holidays are available all over the world but for most of the British, Spain is their chosen golfing destination. There are those who believe that learning golf is best practised and understood in a relaxed and warm environment away from the stresses of everyday life. The beauty of golf is that it can be enjoyed by anyone, no matter what their age . . . it's never too late to learn to play. It is a good way of keeping active during retirement plus it is a rewarding, often frustrating and, to some, highly addictive game.

The Costa del Golf

The Costa del Sol is also known as the Costa del Golf and if you are planning to retire to Spain, purchasing a Spanish villa on a golf course makes sound investment sense. It also makes sense to look for a development where the golf is not overwhelmed by the residential side of the development and equally where the residential development is not 'dwarfed' by the golf course.

Membership of a Spanish golf club

Some Spanish developments include the automatic right of all purchasers to apply for membership to the golf club. This does not mean that membership is included in the purchase price. Membership is often quite costly, on top of which there will also be an annual fee. If you are planning to retire to Spain in the future and need to rent out your villa until retirement, then golf can afford you the luxury of winter lets, as well as the normal seasonal lets. Always check that the club has facilities for non-members before making your purchase. Golfing developments, especially those with a track record and extensive facilities such as concierge services, tennis, riding facilities, plus a luxurious spa and five star hotels, offer an element of security as an investment. They will always have appeal to those who are relocating, retirees, holiday makers and regular golf enthusiasts.

Getting started

Golf is a remarkably easy game to learn and enjoy. The biggest mistake made by people wanting to get started is to rush out and buy a brand new set of shiny and expensive golf clubs. While they are nice to look at, you should keep in mind that today's golf equipment comes in great varieties to cater for different golfing types and abilities. Since you're just starting out, you do not know which set fits you best. So, if you invest heavily in the wrong set of golf clubs, you will either have to sell them at a greatly reduced price or compromise your game. If you feel you must own your own clubs, purchase just a few basic irons, woods, a putter and a wedge. These clubs are more than enough to get you started. Alternatively, try hiring them from a driving range.

In the beginning

The golf course is not the place to learn to play golf. Your first port of call is a driving range. Golf is technically quite demanding and without at least some basic training, you'll end up frustrated. You will most likely never get a ball even near a hole and other people, having to wait for you, will also not be happy. So the rule is to take at least four or five lessons from a professional, learn the fundamentals, progress to a 9 hole course and eventually venture out into the great unknown of an 18 hole golf course. It will be a lot more fun for you, and those around you, if you follow this path.

How else can I learn?

In addition to lessons, which should be from a professional from the PGA (see below) books and videos can be invaluable in learning the basics. To build a sound golf swing you will need to know the three fundamentals: grip, stance and posture. There are some very good books and videos on the market that will help you to establish the three fundamentals.

Professional Golfers Association (PGA)

If you are keen to learn how to play, you should contact your local PGA as they will be able to advise you on suitable courses and instructors in your area. The PGA was founded in 1901 and has continued to develop steadily over the years. The PGA has over 5,000 qualified professionals, who employ approximately 1,000 registered trainees. There are seven regional headquarters located throughout Great Britain and Ireland which have full time staff available for advice on all aspects of the game. The regional offices also organise their own tournament circuits. The PGA is constantly striving to improve its services to members and their status in the wider world of golf.

Information

For information on municipal golf courses and private clubs, contact the National Golf Club Unions. They can also provide information on adult education centres and sports clubs that offer courses for beginners and improvers:

◆ English Golf Union: 01526 354500 or www.englishgolfunion.org.
◆ Golfing Union of Ireland: 00 353 269 4111 or www.gui.ie.
◆ Scottish Golf Union: 01382 549500 or www.scottishgolf.org.
◆ Welsh Golfing Union: 01633 430830 or www.welshgolf.org.

LADIES GOLF

Women are not welcome at some golf courses, but there really is no reason why this game cannot be enjoyed by both sexes. If you want to learn golf there are, as well as lessons, golf holidays. Some of which cater exclusively to women. The best place to source these holidays is to look on the Internet to find out what is available. As an example 'Rufflets Country House Hotel' in Scotland offers:

Go Girl Programme: Introduction to golf: three day golf school.

> Learn the basics of the game with grip, swing, posture and develop the right approach and expectations. Price (currently £250.00 per person) includes lunch, refreshments, club hire, workbook, practise programme, driving range balls, green fees on Balgove course (nine holes).

For information contact: Rufflets Country House Hotel, tel: 01334 472594 or e-mail: reservations@rufflets.co.uk.

Ladies Golf Union (LGU)

The LGU was founded in 1893 and is the governing body for Ladies' Amateur Golf in Great Britain and Ireland. The business of the LGU is conducted by an executive council made up of two lady representatives each from England, Ireland, Scotland and Wales. Whilst policy is set by the Executive Council, a team of nine staff run the business on a day-to-day basis.

Holidays for lady golfers in Thailand

Thailand is rapidly emerging as a 'Golfing Paradise for Ladies', not just because of its wide range of international courses and facilities, but also thanks to all those other pluses that ladies enjoy including fabulous spas, world-class cuisine and lots of value-for-money shopping. Plus, and it's a big plus, . . . there's little discrimination there. Ladies are very welcome. Clubhouses have changing facilities for ladies, spas and beauty salons, pleasant 19th hole refreshment areas and often a lively karaoke room. You don't even have to be a member to play at most clubs. There are more than 100 international standard golf courses in Thailand, concentrated around the major tourist destinations of Bangkok, Phuket, Pattaya, Hua Hin, Chiang Mai and Kanchanaburi. Caddies are Thailand's best-kept golfing secret. They ensure the smooth running of Thailand's golf courses and 95% of them are female.

The Thailand Amateur Ladies Golf Association (TALGA)

The facilities for lady golfers can trace their beginnings back to 1978 when various clubs bonded together to form, what is now called, TALGA. Its prime objective was to raise the standards of ladies golf in Thailand so they could compete internationally. In doing so, they focused attention on golf facilities for ladies, encouraging standards to be raised at courses as well. For further information tel: Bangkok (662) 261 5116-8 or visit www.thaigolfer.com.

Coco Golf

This company has been organising golf tours from the UK to Thailand for the past 12 years, usually for mixed groups and couples from UK golf clubs. A typical 12-day tour costs around £1,000, inclusive of flights, accommodation, breakfasts, transfers and six rounds of golf. For further information contact: Coco Golf Thailand, Tel: 0207 193 3355 or e-mail: simon@cocogolf.net. Other websites offering information on golf in Thailand incude: www.siamgolfbiz.com or www.golforient.com.

SAILING

The idea of sitting on the deck of your own boat sailing through the crystal blue waters towards some tropical island is the stuff of true retirement fantasy – for men at least. You only need to go to the Boat Show and watch grown men reduced to gibbering wrecks as they reach for their cheque books. Unfortunately very few women really enjoy sailing and partners rarely make good sailing companions. Tempers get frayed, fear sets in as the reality is very often long nights in stormy seas, with no adequate mooring and a condensation soaked sleeping bag. That's before I've mentioned the toilet arrangements! 50% of boats are never taken out of the marina from one year to the next and the reason that is often quoted is 'the wife didn't like it'. The advice here is very simple: don't rush in and 'Spend The Kids' Inheritance' and buy a boat just because you've got the money, time on your hands and have always dreamt of doing it. Stop and wait!

The practical approach

Sailing is a great hobby if you go about it properly. If you haven't done much sailing the best thing is to go on a course – preferably with your partner if you want to sail together. There are two types of sailing: dinghy and yachting. There are lots of courses up and down the country. They are not expensive and you can get a good holiday out of it as well. Read the sailing magazines or look on the Internet for suitable courses but make sure that they are RYA qualified. This is not always vital, but it does provide a seal of approval. They also offer qualifications which are internationally recognised. This will be useful when hiring a boat and getting insurance. The law does not require you to have any qualifications at all to take a non-commercial boat out to sea, but only a fool would take any type of boat out without knowing what they were doing as the sea can be a very dangerous place!

Learning to sail dinghies

This can be done on reservoirs, lakes or the sea. It's merely a question of finding somewhere that is suitable for you. All courses are run by enthusiasts and they get as big a kick as you as you become more adept.

Getting wet

You will capsize and you will get wet. These days there are good, cheap wet suits and dry suits so basically you can sail in any weather. Of course it's more pleasant in the summer. We have been on sailing courses in Ireland, Turkey and Greece and the whole family has had a lot of fun. I think that doing a full week's course on holiday is the best way to learn – preferably somewhere hot!

Sailing holidays

Check the sailing magazines for courses in your area. Two big international operators are Sunsail and Mark Warner. They have beach clubs which offer good accommodation, food and a whole range of water sports. They have a full complement of dinghies which willing young gap year students pull in and out of the water for you. It's a very painless and fun way to learn how to sail. To contact Sunsail tel: 0870 428 4146 or visit www.sunsail.com. To contact Mark Warner tel: 0870 770 4228 or visit www.markwarner.co.uk. Both companies offer good last minute deals. Holidays outside of school holidays are obviously much cheaper and if your partner doesn't enjoy sailing, there are plenty of activities for them to do on shore . . . including just relaxing by the pool!

Buying a dinghy

Having tried lots of different dinghies, you'll have a better idea of the type that you best enjoy sailing. If you have got the 'bug', buying a dinghy is relatively inexpensive. You can buy new or second hand – it just depends on your pocket. There are plenty of good used dinghies on the market, as yet again, people buy boats in a fit of enthusiasm and then don't use them very often. One of the main problems with dinghy sailing is getting someone to crew for you, when you want to go sailing. So, again, do your research and think it through and ask yourself do you genuinely have people who will crew regularly for you? If not, go for a single hander and then you can please yourself.

Buying a new boat

If you want to buy a new boat there is the Dinghy Show which is held at Alexandra Palace, north London each spring. There is also the Boat Show, held at Excel in Docklands every January and Southampton in September. You can get special 'show bargains' but check out prices before you go.

Buying a used boat

Buying a used boat is much easier now and you will save a great deal of money. You will be able to get a dinghy that is in good condition for a lot less than buying new. As with a car, these boats are kept out in all weathers and very quickly lose their shiny finish. The best way to buy is to check the notice board of the club that you would like to join. If you can find a suitable boat – especially one that a senior member of the club is trying to sell – you could get sponsored for membership and if you push hard enough you may get to keep the boat in its existing space, i.e. nearer the water. Boats are heavy to drag uphill so it's important to get a good spot! Also, if problems occur with the boat you've got the previous owner on hand for advice.

Buying a boat on the Internet

If you can't find a boat at the club, the Internet has lots of sites for selling used boats. Make sure you have a good inspection of the boat before buying and, if in doubt, take a friend with you who has experience of buying a boat. Try to take it for a test sail to make sure there are no hidden snags and, more importantly, that you enjoy sailing the boat.

Where to sail?

The other element to think through is where are you going to keep your boat? Obviously this should be within easy distance of home, but will you get bored of going round the same gravel pit? Is it worth travelling a bit further to a huge reservoir or even go a bit further to the sea?

Where to keep the boat

You will also probably want to keep the boat at the place of sailing rather than trailer it around, so you will need to join a sailing club, preferably with people that you like and also where you can get your boat in and out of the water without too much hard work. Sailing clubs are very sociable places and if you want to meet other members then the best way is to race. They usually have a mid-week evening race and a weekend race. All good fun . . . depending on how competitive you want to be!

YACHTING

This is a bit more grown up – and you don't get so wet! It can be monumentally expensive although it doesn't have to be. Especially if you don't rush off and buy a yacht at the Boat Show!

Learning the ropes

Again you need to learn the basics. If you've sailed dinghies you'll know quite a lot but obviously the kit is different and you'll need to find your way around. There are many courses available which offer RYA qualifications. The grades are: competent crew, day skipper, coastal skipper and yachtmaster, which is a commercial skipper's ticket. These courses cost about £300 per week (excluding fares, food and drink) which isn't bad for a week's sailing, plus you get the added bonus that the skipper will do the cooking as well! There are plenty of courses advertised in sailing magazines for the UK and abroad. You could get a cheap flight to Gibraltar and sail around the Mediterranean, go to the Greek Islands or try out one of the Sunsail resorts. All of these are good value and very sociable.

The route to experience

The entry level is competent crew, which is exactly what it says. Generally a week of living on the yacht and sailing with other people doing the skippers course. This is a good course to test out how keen your partner may or may not be about the whole sailing concept.

- **Day skipper**: a two week course. The first week is theory – navigation, tides, weather, etc. The second week is practical – handling the boat and using your theory. This enables you to sail within sight of the coastline.
- **Coastal skipper**: another two week course. The same subjects are covered as day skipper, but in greater detail. This enables you to sail 60 miles out.
- **Yachtmaster**: a 14 week commercial qualification and by the end of it you can sail across oceans and take fee paying passengers.

Other courses

There are other day courses available in radio, engine maintenance, radar, GPS systems, etc. With a day skipper qualification you will be well equipped to take a yacht out on your own.

Getting a crew

However, the perennial problem of sailing a yacht is that you cannot really do it alone. If you are piddling about in waters you know very well and the boat is not too big, you can sail with just one other person, provided they know what they are doing. It's best to sail with at least three people on board. If you are planning overnight trips, you will need two watches so that equates to about four people. The problem, as ever, is have you got access to this number of people? If not, your boat is going to sit idle in the marina.

Sailing without buying a boat

So, you've done the courses. Do you need to buy a boat of your own? As we've seen those who've bought boats are having enough problems finding a crew – why not crew for them? You can have all the fun and none of the expense! This is a great way to enjoy sailing without busting your bank balance and 'Spending The Kids' Inheritance'. Plus you can sail on a whole range of boats, all over the world and join in ocean races like the ARC – the Azores to Antigua – on someone else's boat. The sailing magazines have adverts and if you search on Google on the Internet 'sailing crew wanted' you can take your pick.

Chartering

Your RYA qualifications are internationally recognised and, as such, you will be able to charter a yacht anywhere in the world. Again consult the yachting magazines or the Internet, as there are thousands of companies and individuals chartering boats. Choose a well established company and don't go for the cheapest. The advantage of chartering is that you can pick up the boat where you want to – preferably somewhere warm – without having the slog of getting the boat there. Also if there are any problems, it's up to the charter company to sort them out.

If you want to buy a boat

I have been assuming that your partner does not share your enthusiasm for your new found hobby. But, if by some lucky chance, you both like sailing then why not buy a boat? You can go on trips together, sail down to hotter climes or even go across the Atlantic. All these journeys can be done in stages. Leave the boat in a marina, come home and then go out again to complete the next leg of your journey. Fabulous!

What sort of boat to buy?

By now you will have sailed a lot of boats and will have an idea of the type and size of boat that appeals to you. Buying a new boat is expensive but it's your retirement . . . so why not? Or buy a used boat that has been well cared for and has all the modern kit. You could even go for a labour of love that needs totally rebuilding or buy a share in a boat. A quarter share lets you use it once every four weeks. Is that, in reality, enough?

Professional survey

By now you are armed with more knowledge to make a proper value judgement. Whatever you do, when you've found the boat of your dreams, get a professional survey done before you buy.

The other half

Just in case you are wondering, the above section on sailing was written by my husband . . . it's his passion (not mine) in case you couldn't tell!

SWIMMING

Is a great way of keeping fit and some local authorities have designated pool times reserved exclusively for older people. If you have never learned to swim or just want to improve your skills, you can also get lessons. For further information contact the Amateur Swimming Association (ASA): tel: 0871 200 0928 or visit www.britishswimming.org.

SO YOU WANT TO GO FISHING?

There are two types of fishing to choose from: coarse fishing and fly fishing. You can fish in rivers, canals, reservoirs or the sea. *Fishing for Dummies* is a good book to start with and is available from all of the online bookstores. It gives you simple instructions, terms, definitions and generally points you in the right direction. Alternatively, you could enquire about tuition from the Professional Anglers Association: tel: 01386 554677 or visit www.paauk.com. The PAA can provide expert tuition for all ages and abilities and will be able to advise where to fish in your area. They can also offer group and family tuition and corporate fishing days.

TENNIS

Tennis is a great way of keeping fit. It does not have to be played to Wimbledon standards and if you want to enjoy a relaxing game of tennis, you should be able easily to find a partner at your local tennis club who would be on a par with you. If you have never played tennis before (and even if you have) then you may benefit from some coaching. If you contact The Lawn Tennis Association they should be able to advise you: tel: 0207 381 7052 or visit www.lta.org.uk.

Tennis for people with disabilities

The British Tennis Foundation oversees and develops tennis opportunities for people with disabilities. The BTF is housed within the LTA. There are introductory camps for people in wheelchairs or with deaf and learning disabilities. One great thing for people with disabilities playing tennis is that there are very few changes to the conventional game and this makes it very attractive. For wheelchair tennis, there is a two bounce rule. In deaf tennis competitions, hearing aids are removed to make it a level platform. All equipment is used and the size of the courts are the same as able bodied tennis. Everyone progresses to play tennis to their ability and not their disability. Visit www.btf.org.uk.

BOWLING

The English Bowling Association was founded in 1903 and is a well organised sport which hosts numerous competitions from clubs to national level. Because success in bowling doesn't require physical fitness, it is particularly favoured by older people but it is becoming increasingly popular with younger players too. Bowls historians believe that the game developed from the Egyptians. One of their pastimes was to play skittles with round stones and from this occupation, it is believed, developed the game of bowls that we know today.

Bowls for beginners

The game of bowls is played on a 34 to 40 metre square of closely cut grass called the green. The green is divided into playing areas called rinks. The green is surrounded by a small ditch to catch bowls which leave the green, and a bank upon which markers indicate the corners and centre lines of each rink. Players deliver their bowls alternately from a mat at one end of the rink towards a small white ball, called 'the jack' at the other end. The bowls are shaped so that they do not run in a straight line but take a curved path towards 'the jack'. To be successful the bowls must be delivered with the correct weight, along the correct line and they can be delivered either forehand or backhand. Bowls can be played as single player, or in teams of pairs, triples, or fours. For more information on bowling and The English Bowling Association for both men and women, visit www.bowlsengland.com or contact your local bowling club.

SUMMARY

Isolation can often creep up on people in their later years and it can rob the mind of the stimulation it needs to stay in tip-top form. Taking up a sport can be a good way to meet people and an enjoyable way of getting gentle exercise. Medical research has found that contact with friends and relatives and keeping up social activities has a significant effect in protecting against mental decline in the elderly. According to research from the University of Michigan, it is the number of friends that you have and not the amount of money you have, that will predict how happy you will be in your later years. It seems that social activities and having friends really can protect you from the effects of the wear and tear of life. Of course, you don't actually have to be a sports fanatic to gain these benefits. Any regular social events will produce the same results. For example, a bridge club or a book club would all provide the benefits of friendship and mental stimulation. So if you want to retire and make the most of life, taking up some form of physical or mental exercise will help give you a focus. It doesn't mean that you will have to 'Spend The Kids' Inheritance', but if that's what you want to do visit www.luxurylifestyle.com for further ideas.

Retirement Homes and Holiday Lets

If you are planning to retire to an area of natural beauty and are wanting to purchase a home before your retirement, you may find that buying your retirement home now and renting it out on a 'holiday let' basis until you are ready to live there, may be a way of having your cake and eating it. The beauty of holiday lets is that you can enjoy holidays in your future home, whilst at the same time, generating an income towards its cost. There are several tax advantages to owning a holiday home that you are renting out and these tax incentives may make the proposition of owning a second home financially viable for you (see The Tax Situation at the end of this chapter).

LOCATION

As with all property, the location of your retirement/holiday home will be an important consideration, from a rental point of view. You will want it to be in an area that has some tourist appeal, otherwise people will not want to holiday there. If the area you want to retire to is totally remote and a considerable distance from any attractions, it may not be suitable for holiday lets. So consider very carefully exactly what the primary purpose of owning a second home will be, before you purchase. You may also want to consider how practical it would be to retire somewhere that is totally isolated and a distance from local amenities, as it is inevitable that as you get older you may want to be close to help should you need it.

Ideal locations for holiday lets
◆ Near major tourist attractions.
◆ Beauty spots.
◆ Near the coast.
◆ Close to areas of architectural interest.
◆ Close to areas of historical interest.

WHAT TYPE OF HOLIDAY ACCOMMODATION IS MOST SUITABLE FOR LETTING?

The general preference is for cottage type accommodation, which can sleep four to six people. Obviously, the more your property sleeps, the wider your market will be. Larger properties however, that sleep more will put a lot of wear and tear on your appliances and make accidents and breakages more likely to happen. It is also worth considering that retirement is generally a time for downsizing so owning a large second home might have implications for manageability when you retire. Or, you may choose a large place to accommodate family and friends, with the plan that you may downsize later and buy a smaller retirement home in the same area.

Holiday letting companies

It is the job of a holiday letting company to obtain clients on your behalf. If the holiday letting company is well established, it will no doubt produce a colour brochure each year, advertising the properties it has registered with them. It will send these brochures out, not only to new clients but also to its existing client database. New clients will be generated from sources such as advertising campaigns in magazines, guidebooks and, more importantly these days, on the Internet. The website of any holiday letting company should show a full range of properties, searchable by location, size and price and should invite enquiries by e-mail. If you are thinking of using the services of one of these companies check out their website first, to see if you like the presentation.

How does it work?

Bookings are accepted from clients in accordance with terms and conditions, which will be set out by the individual holiday company. Some companies offer a full management service, which will take care of all aspects of running the holiday let business for you. Expect to pay a considerable amount for this, in the region of 40 to 50% of the anticipated holiday rental, as this will not only have to cover agency fees but also all the caretaker/cleaning expenses. Other companies operate as a letting agent and will generally charge 20% of the holiday rental plus VAT. It will be their job to offer out your property and to take bookings on your behalf.

Bookings

Bookings are accepted from clients in accordance with the agreement between the owner and the holiday company. All bookings should be confirmed in writing to you and the client, once the client's deposit payment has been received. Full payment of the rent due, plus details of the booking are sent to owners about two to three weeks before the start of each holiday, together with, if possible, the clients anticipated arrival time. Clients are provided with details of the property, comprehensive directions, and detailed arrangements for key collection. Telephone numbers of owners/caretakers are provided with this package, to enable clients to communicate any last minute change of arrival times or unexpected delays. This procedure could differ slightly, depending on which holiday company you choose to use.

Cancellation insurance

Most holiday companies will offer cancellation insurance, which will enable clients to get some, if not all, of their money back in the unhappy event that they have to cancel their holiday. If the agency works in conjunction with other agencies in the EU, the regulations may differ slightly but offer much the same benefits. It is becoming increasingly common that clients have their own annual travel insurance policies. It is up to the holiday company to check that the cover provided is adequate and, if it is not, they should inform clients of their obligations to pay the rent in full, if they have to cancel and the property cannot be re-let.

Property insurance

Most domestic buildings and contents policies do not provide insurance cover when the property is used for holiday lettings, they certainly do not provide cover for the loss of income, should your property need to be repaired and is inaccessible or otherwise out of use. Most holiday companies will have contacts with specialist insurers who deal with issues relating to holiday lets. Ask your holiday company for their details.

Diary of bookings

It will also be necessary for tax purposes to have an up-to-date diary of bookings and visitors details and you will need to keep these details for a minimum of 12 months.

ACCOMMODATION QUALITY ASSESSMENT

Hotel and guest accommodation proprietors can choose to have their establishments assessed by one of the three national organisations, in order to receive either a star rating (hotels) or a diamond rating (guest accommodation). The English Tourism Council, the AA and RAC all offer this service, which involves the completion by you, of an assessment application form and payment of a fee (dependent on the size of the property). An assessor will then visit your property to establish the number of stars/diamonds you are eligible for.

Accreditation

If you are going to be running your holiday letting business yourself this will be a useful rating to include in your brochure. If you are using an established holiday company this may not be as necessary, as a representative of the company will have visited your property and made their own assessment. They will base their advertising upon this. Most companies that do their own assessment should be recognised by The English Association of Self Catering Operators (EASCO) visit www.englishselfcatering.co.uk. Check with the holiday company that they are recognised by this authority. Other authorities include:

- The Association of Scotland's Self Caterers (ASSC): www.assc.co.uk.
- The Wales Association of Self Catering Operators (WASCO): www.walescottages.org.uk.
- The Northern Ireland Self Catering Holiday Association (NISCHA): www.nischa.com.

Fire safety

Contact your local fire brigade safety officer to check that you comply with fire precaution requirements. Broadly these apply to any property capable of sleeping over six people (excluding yourself and your family).

THE DIY APPROACH TO HOLIDAY LETTING

If you have the time and do not mind answering the phone and doing your own paperwork, you may choose not to use the services of a holiday letting company and save yourself their commission fees. The Internet has made this easier as you can set up your own website about your property. You will, however, need to have a brochure printed, as you will need to send this out to prospective clients. This should contain comprehensive and accurate details about your property. Remember it is the property you are trying to sell to your clients, not necessarily the area, as they will most probably have decided on where they want to holiday before they approach you.

Be accurate with your property description

Do not make claims in your brochure that are not accurate, as you do not want a disgruntled holidaymaker who has had their holiday ruined because you have not been entirely truthful about your property. When designing your brochure/flyer, always print your seasonal rates on a separate piece of paper and include this with your brochure. The reason for this is that your rates will change each year and you do not want the expense of printing out your brochure annually!

Setting the weekly rate

Check with your local tourist board what the rates are for properties in similar areas and take into account seasonal variations. The rates you charge will have no effect on the classification and grading.

Reservation fee

Always ask for a non-fundable reservation fee. This should be 25% of the holiday rental. Once you have received this and you have cleared funds in your bank account you can send the client confirmation of their booking. With this confirmation you will need to send an invoice for the balance due. Confirm that you will need this to be paid in full,

28 days before the holiday is due to commence. If payment is not received by this date then you will be entitled to keep the reservation deposit as a cancellation fee.

When the balance is received

When sending the receipt, inform the client of the key collection arrangements and the time that they can enter the property. If you have agreed to charge for certain extras and have arranged for a damage deposit to be paid, always ask for these to be paid in cash on arrival. This saves funds having to be cleared and, in the event of a cancellation, funds having to be returned.

Cancellations

You will need to set out your requirements for this in your terms and conditions, which will be included in your brochure. It is important that all your documentation states exactly what your terms and conditions are. This can be done as a simple footer on the bottom of all receipts and invoices, for example. It is inevitable that cancellations will happen at sometime but it is unusual for these to happen after the full balance has been paid. If this does happen, it will generally be for a reason that is covered by insurance and you should not find yourself short of funds. It is always a good idea to make holiday insurance a necessity of the booking conditions. You can include this in your terms and conditions.

How long is the holiday season?

The holiday season in the right property, in the right location, can be almost all year round. This may not involve the property being let all the time at the peak summer rate, but it could involve long weekend breaks, which are becoming more and more popular. Christmas, New Year, Easter and the Spring Bank holiday weekend, although technically out of season, are all popular times for letting and generally carry a price premium.

- Low season: January, February, March.
- Mid season: April, May, June, September, October, November December.
- High season: July and August.

Council tax/water rates/utility bills

You will be responsible for paying these bills in the usual way. Local councils offer a 10% discount on the council tax of a property which is classified as a second home.

Caretakers/key holders

This is the most difficult area to get right when letting out a holiday cottage and it is important (if you are not available to do this yourself or don't want to do it) that you employ a trustworthy and reliable caretaker for the property. The caretaker will be the first point of contact your guests will have when they arrive at the property.

Changeovers

The changeover is the time between one set of visitors leaving and another arriving. The departure time is usually 10am and the arrival time after 2:30pm. The time in between is used for the changeover which involves:

- Change of linen.
- Full clean of property.
- Minor repairs.
- Providing towels (if hired).
- Erecting cot (if hired).
- Cleaning windows.
- Gardening duties (if applicable).
- If there are any breakages, sorting out replacement items.

Granny's cast offs

If the property is well presented and is not full of Granny's 'cast offs', the chances are that your guests will do their best to keep the property in good order too. If the furnishings are tatty and the plates are chipped, you have only got yourself to blame if the property is left in a mess!

What written information should I leave about the Property?

◆ Your own and/or your local key holders phone numbers for emergencies.
◆ Where to find: spare lamp bulbs, emergency lighting (i.e. torches), meters, fuse box, and earth trip switch, water stopcock.
◆ Notes on refuse collection day and where to put the refuse for collection.
◆ Inventory/help lists.

Help lists

For the convenience of your clients, leave help lists over the appliances. This will save them having to plough through complicated instruction manuals and it will also hopefully reduce the chance of damage to your appliances through misuse.

Useful information about the area

You should leave information for your clients on the following:

◆ local accident and emergency hospital
◆ doctor
◆ vet (if animals are accepted in your property)
◆ nearest pay-phone
◆ local shops for milk, newspapers and groceries (with opening times if possible)
◆ pubs, wine bars, restaurants, takeaways
◆ supermarket
◆ churches (various religions)

- information/leaflets on local places of interest
- nearest public transport
- taxi firms
- local maps with details of footpaths, walks, cycle routes, etc.

Leave your client a comprehensive list of what the area has to offer and present it neatly in a folder to be left in the property. This will not only help your guests get the most out of their stay, it will also encourage them to come back again. Remember, repeat business is the life and soul of holiday letting!

Visitors with disabilities

Disability does not necessarily mean wheelchair access and there are many things that should be done and could be done to help people who are disabled in any way. Call the Disability Discrimination Act on tel: 08457 622 633 or visit www.drc.org.uk/whatwedo/guestacom.asp, for up-to-date guidelines and regulations.

IS THERE A DOWNSIDE TO HOLIDAY LETTING?

The biggest drawback to a holiday let is that you will most likely not be able to use your property when you would like to. High season is the most popular time and that is when you will be able to charge a premium for your property. If you want to use it during the summer months, this will not only be uneconomical but will also jeopardise your relationship with your holiday company (if you choose to use one). They will not want to spend money advertising the property if is not available at peak times. This does not mean that you can't use your property at all during the popular months, it just means that you will have to be reasonable with your requests. You will also have to formally book your time, as the holiday company will need to know when you intend to use the property yourself, in order to avoid double bookings. Holiday lets differ from standard lets as your client's expectations will be higher. They will have spent a long time deciding where to go and will probably have booked their holiday accommodation well in advance. It is important that when they arrive everything is clean and welcoming. You would hate to be responsible for ruining someone's hard earned holiday!

THE TAX SITUATION

If you let out a furnished holiday home it is counted as a trade by the tax authorities. This means there are some useful tax advantages to be had, as it qualifies for 'Business Asset Taper Relief' amongst other things. In order to qualify, the following criteria must be met:

- The property must be furnished.
- It must be available for commercial letting for at least 140 days in a 12 month period.
- It must be let out for at least 70 days in a 12 month period.
- It must not be let out to the same occupants for more than 31 days consecutively at any time during a period of 7 months out of the same 12 month period as above.
- The property must be in the UK.
- The 12 month period is usually the tax year.

Income tax

Income tax is paid on profits. That is after all expenses, including mortgage payments, agent's commission, property maintenance and council tax etc. have been deducted from the moneys received. Unlike buy to let, losses can be charged against the owner's profits on their other business.

VAT

VAT is not chargeable on rents. For income tax purposes the gross amount of expenses, including the VAT element, should be claimed.

Capital Gains Tax

As the holiday let qualifies as a 'business asset' for CGT, like commercial property, it qualifies for business asset taper relief, which is more advantageous than relief on residential property.

Property held for less than one year	Nil
Property held for one year but less than two years	50%
Property held for two years or more	75%

Holiday lets abroad

Each country has different rules and regulations for paying tax on earnings and capital gains from holiday lets. Before buying a property ensure that you have researched the relevant tax regulations, as these can be very onerous.

SUMMARY

As retirement opportunities expand and property increases in value, it may well be prudent to buy now, as opposed to waiting until you are actually retired. Even if you decide that you do not want to retire to your holiday home, it is unlikely that you will have lost money (unless of course you bought ill advisedly or paid over the odds) and you should be able to sell at a profit, which will contribute to your pension plans.

Staying Put or Moving On?

There may come a time when you will need to decide whether you want to stay in your own home or move to a more manageable place, be it assisted or independent living. If you are lucky and enjoying good health, you may not need to make any changes to your home environment, but often this is not the case. If you are becoming less mobile, there are organisations and grants available that can help you adapt your home to your changing needs if you wish to stay put.

With advancements in technology the world is changing fast and it may not be long before we see 'computerised health centres' in the home.

On a daily basis, a person could slip a finger or hand into contact with 'sensors' that could measure vital signs such as blood pressure, glucose levels and oxygen saturation in the blood. This information could be instantaneously transmitted to a doctor's office, prompting a call from health care workers if anything is not as it should be. Similar technology could ensure that the proper medications have been taken at the right time.

Keeping the elderly in their own homes where possible is the way forward and more cost effective than being institutionalised. The next section of the book aims to explore ways in which you can 'stay put'.

ELDERLY ACCOMMODATION COUNSEL

This organisation provides information about specialist housing and care provision for the elderly. It is based in London and provides a UK-wide service. The phone line is operated between the hours of 9 am to 5 pm, monday to friday. For further information tel: 0207 820 1343 or visit www.housingcare.org.uk.

What services do they offer?

They offer help and advice on four main areas:

- Remaining at home, accessing support and care for staying put.
- Moving to more suitable housing.
- Moving to a care environment.
- Paying for any of the above.

The service does not provide home visits and can only be contacted by phone, post or e-mail. It will also provide general information regarding financial issues, but for any specific help you will need to contact the Financial Services Authority (see Chapter 7 on Finance).

Adapting the home

The first priority in adapting any home is safety. Although it is impossible to fully prevent all accidents, it is imperative to take an objective look at your home, particularly in relation to what might trigger a fall. A fall in later life can often be fatal, as it can lead to so many other things. Failing eyesight (an 85 year old needs three times the light that a 15 year old needs) and loss of balance make older people more prone to falling. This can result in broken bones which the ageing population is particularly susceptible to. Bone density decreases with age and fractures can easily occur, leading to lifelong disabilities. The reasons for these falls can be varied and some of them are listed below:

- medication
- pain/worry/anxiety
- inadequate food and liquid intake
- weak muscles
- failing eyesight/new glasses
- polished floors/variations in walking surfaces
- new shoes/unsteady gait
- fatigue.

HOME SWEET HOME

The reasons people choose to stay in their own homes for as long as possible is that they are surrounded by things they know and enjoy living in a community which is familiar to them. If you are keen to stay in your present home, you should contact your local social services department to ask for an assessment of your needs. It could be that you may need care in the home, special equipment, 'meals on wheels' or visits to a day centre. You can also contact your local Age Concern to find out about social activities, visiting schemes and information services. Other things to consider are:

- Contacting the pensions service to check that you are receiving all the benefits you are entitled to.
- Contact your local GP about home visits from the district nurse, health visitor and chiropodist.
- Installing a community alarm system, so that you can call for help 24 hours a day. By pressing a button on a pendant, or pulling a cord, a message is relayed to a monitoring centre.
- Contacting a local Home Improvement Agency/Care & Repair or Staying Put Agency.
- Contact the crime prevention officer for advice on security.
- If you want to enjoy some of the benefits of having some spare cash to spend, then releasing equity in your home for a more comfortable retirement (see Chapter 7 on Finance).

PRACTICAL SOLUTIONS

If there is no downstairs cloakroom, you will need to find a way to adapt a room so that it can be converted for this use. Elderly people increasingly find stairs difficult and this adaptation is not only useful, but also a necessary addition to any modern household. So, rather than consider it an expense, see it as an investment. You can of course apply to your local council regarding any adaptations, as certain grants might be available. If there is no room on the ground floor of your accommodation to convert, you may have to consider installing a stair lift. However, there are many ways that a home can be adapted to meet changing needs and not all of them involve complicated adaptations. Often a practical solution can be found regarding the problem.

- Keep the vacuum cleaner downstairs and have a simple carpet sweeper upstairs. This will save lugging a heavy item up and down the stairs.
- Look at storage. How can things be improved? Are certain items stored too high, or are they stored too low, resulting in you having to

reach and bend? Keep items that are used on a daily basis more accessible and within easy reach.

◆ Kitchen safety. There are many gadgets on the market to help in the kitchen.

◆ Buy a microwave as it is easy to operate and can be a useful aid to cooking, particularly if the oven controls are difficult to manage (although special controls can be obtained).

◆ Door knobs. You can change these for levers or place a sleeve on the knob itself making it easier to grip.

◆ Electric sockets can easily be raised to waist height. Plugs can be purchased with handgrips.

◆ If you are constantly packing the ironing board away . . . keep it open and store it away in a spare room.

◆ Grab rails can be fitted in the bathroom, stairs or anywhere you may need extra support. Contact your local Age Concern to enquire about whether they offer this as part of their 'handyman' service.

INSULATION IN THE HOME

As you will be spending a lot more time in your home after retirement, you will be using a lot more energy in respect of heating. It may be worth considering improving the insulation in the house. Most of the heat escapes through the roof, walls, doors and windows. There are grants available to help with this and it is worth contacting Environmental Health or the housing department of your local council for an application form for home repair assistance. Alternatively you can apply for a grant, if you are over 60, to make your home more energy efficient, by contacting the Home Energy Efficiency Scheme on tel: 0800 952 0600 or www.adviceguide.org. If you are going to employ someone to insulate the loft for you, contact the National Association of Loft Insulation Contractors on tel: 01428 654011 or visit www.dubois.vital.co.uk. If you are considering insulating your loft yourself, contact Age Concern to ask for advice. Also available from

Age Concern is their fact sheet *Help with Heating*. Tel: 0800 009966 for further information.

STAIR LIFTS

Here are some points you may like to consider when choosing a stair lift:

- Cheapest is not necessarily the best and in many cases you pay for what you get.
- Is the chair as easy and as safe to get on at the top of the stairs as it is at the bottom?
- What happens if there is a power cut? Is there a manual lowering device?
- Is the battery drive unit easy to purchase through the contractor and how long do the batteries last?
- What is the cost of replacement batteries and other services?
- How long is the warranty and what does it cover?
- Do you have to pay any money up front with the order and, if you do, why should you? It is preferable to pay on completion or at least when the chair is first installed and is operational.
- Can you rent or lease the stair lift?
- What are the maintenance charges?
- Can you get a guaranteed buy back clause should you decide to sell your house and no longer need the stair lift?
- Is it comfortable to ride in?
- Does it complement your existing décor as much as possible? Remember you will have to live with it!
- Do your stairs have a bend or a curve? If so, you will have to opt for a custom built option, but again this will probably be cheaper than moving house.

Independent advice

If you are considering the purchase of a stair lift make sure you get independent advice from an occupational therapist or The Disabled Living Foundation advice department. Tel: 0845 130 9177 or visit www.dlf.org.uk.

How can I fund all the improvements necessary for 'staying put'?

If your home could do with a substantial upgrade and you own it, you may consider re-mortgaging. This means using some of the equity out of your home to fund the cost of the improvements (see Chapter 7 on Finance). Age Concern publishes a factsheet on this issue called *Raising Income or Capital from your Home*. Contact Age Concern: tel 0800 00 99 66.

Where do I get advice from about home improvements?

All councils have environmental officers with responsibilities for disrepair and poor conditions in private housing and there is usually a specialist housing person or section. Councils also provide grants for repair and improvement works, although these are limited and means tested. You may also qualify for a disabled facilities grant. Contact Disability Alliance on tel: 0207 247 8776 for their book *The Disability Rights Handbook*. There is a cost for this book or alternatively your local library should have a copy. Or visit www.disabilityalliance.org.

If I have difficulty getting out of the bath, can social services help?

Social services can provide advice on the type of equipment and adaptations that should be installed. They may also be able to provide a list of builders, experienced in this field, and perhaps offer reduced prices on equipment and provide information on second hand equipment. Alternatively you can contact your nearest Disabled Living Centre on tel: 0161 834 1044 or visit www.dlcc.org.uk.

Repairs and renovations for council tenants

Your local community housing office will provide advice and assistance.

Repairs and renovations when renting from a housing association

You should contact your Housing Association, as it is responsible for general repairs and maintenance issues.

Adaptations when renting from a private landlord

Contact social services who will visit you in your own home and talk to you about your needs. They will give advice on equipment and adaptations but will require written permission from your landlord before any work can be undertaken. The disability facilities grant is available to cover this work, but it is means tested and you may be asked to contribute to the costs. If you cannot afford to do this, contact social services, who may be able to offer advice about other sources of funding.

PRIMARY CARE SERVICES

These are a range of services that are often based at GP practices. You may need a GP referral to access these services, although for some of them you can refer yourself. These services are all aimed at keeping those in need in their own homes as long as possible.

- care assistants and domestic care
- chiropodists
- community dieticians
- counsellors, psychotherapists and psychologists
- mental health nurses
- district nurses
- occupational therapists
- physiotherapists
- practice/specialist nurses
- speech and language therapists.

NHS Direct

The NHS also has walk in centres and these centres do not require an appointment. They deal with minor illnesses and injuries and are run by nurses. If you are unsure about whether you should call out a GP at night, you can call NHS Direct on the 24-hour help line for advice. Tel: 0845 46 47 or visit www.nhsdirect.nhs.uk.

Ricability

Ricability is an independent research charity that publishes impartial guides for a wide range of equipment and services, which are of use to older and disabled people. As the Research Institute for Consumer Affairs, it also works with manufacturers, regulators and policy makers to improve products and services. For further information, tel: 0207 4272460 or visit www.ricability.org.uk.

SUMMARY

When planning for safety and mobility in the home, it would be wise to consider future needs as well as current ones. Sadly, many older adults who could have otherwise remained independent for years end up in hospitals and nursing homes after falls, which are often the result of poor lighting. Research is being carried out to discover new ways of addressing this problem, such as variable frequency lighting that is automatic, sensitive to motion or to the voice, so that there is no need to fumble for a switch in the middle of the night. Voice activation may soon make it possible to run bath water that is just the right temperature, turn the television on and off and notify the computer to dial a person at home and place them on speaker phone, all without lifting a finger.

Although we do not have this technology widely available yet, we are however, beginning to embrace the concept of 'Lifetime Homes'. They are becoming increasingly popular within the UK and it is clear that there is a demand for homes that can be adapted to changing needs. The concept being, that you do not notice the safety features until you need them. The most important thing to consider when choosing to stay put is how to make your life easy and safe. Age Concern, Help the Aged and social services are all more than happy to help, support and advise you.

MOVING ON

If you have lived in your house for a long time it is most likely dated, cluttered and probably a bit frayed round the edges (no offence) so it will need a bit of organising for it to have the best advantage on the market. This can be true of all family homes to a certain extent, as fashions change and what seemed like a contemporary kitchen five years ago may not look as contemporary now. The same can be said for the internal décor, which as well as general wear and tear, dates very quickly. The first thing you need to do when preparing a property for sale, and before you start on the cosmetic look of the property, is to be able to see what you are doing. That means ridding yourself of clutter!

What is clutter?

Clutter is the stuff you no longer use or care about. It is stuff you liked at one time in your life, but don't like now. It's old paint pots, garden chairs, things stored away because they might come in useful one day. It is also stuff that is no longer any use but may be of use to others . . . so you may be able to do someone a good turn, whilst at the same time helping yourself maximise the selling potential of your home. That is not however, a licence for dumping unwanted goods on (polite) family and friends!

De-cluttering

De-cluttering will have a double impact, on not only helping sell your home, but also in helping you move from it. If you have lived in your home for a long time, it is most probably full of memories, sentimental items and lots of clutter! There will probably be a lot of things belonging to your past that you may find difficult to let go of but if you are moving to a smaller place, there are some things that you quite simply won't have the room for. I recently went through this with my mother who was leaving her four bedroom house for a much smaller two bed apartment. There was a lot of 'stuff' to clear, but it is surprising how therapeutic it can be, sorting out a lifetime of accumulation and only keeping a few items that really matter.

Where do I start?

You may want to make a small beginning, by just sorting through the linen cupboard and bagging up the linen you no longer use and giving it to the charity shop. Empty a cupboard and put everything that you no longer want in a black bin bag. If its good stuff, either sell it or donate it to the charity shop and do this a little at a time. Once you have made a decision to part with something, get it out of the house as soon as possible, so as to avoid any 'change of heart'. If anything is broken that you have been meaning to fix for some time, now is the time to get rid of it. Don't dispose of all sentimental items, but only hold on to those that you really want. Donate unwanted gifts to others and ask people not to buy you presents, as you are in the process of de-cluttering. Buy some storage boxes and throw out any unwanted paperwork and file the rest. Be mindful of 'identity fraud' and make sure that if you do not have a shredder, all documents with personal details on them are thoroughly destroyed.

Once everything is tidy, the house will instantly look better and you may be surprised to find how liberated this makes you feel.

Hanging on to things

If you are completely undecided about letting go of something, store it away somewhere for six months . . . even if it means taking it with you to your new home or putting it into storage. Write the date on it and if you haven't used it or missed it within the six months, then give it away.

Storage

Is not as expensive as it was once was and it may be necessary to store some of your furniture to show the house at its best advantage to potential buyers. It will also make things easier on moving day. However, there is no point in storing something that you are extremely unlikely to use again. So think carefully about what to store, what to sell and what to give away. As for storing personal items whilst you are showing your home, put most personal possessions away in boxes and store them in cupboards, out of the way. For information on storage companies, look in your local telephone directory or *Yellow Pages* or visit www.yell.com.

GIVING THE PROPERTY A FACELIFT

Some friends of mine tried to sell their house recently and failed to find a buyer. I suggested to them that they market the house in the spring and give it a face-lift. The result was that post face-lift the house had an offer put on it within a week for the full asking price and was subsequently sold! It is very important when selling your property that you present it in its best possible light. It does not mean that you shouldn't bother with improvements anymore . . . on the contrary it is exactly the time that you should initiate improvements. Any jobs around the house that need finishing should be completed before you market the property.

A cosmetic refurbishment

As long as the property is structurally sound and the roof is not caving in, it may be possible to change the whole look of a property with very little work having to be done (other than what you can do yourself). A cosmetic refurbishment is not an excuse to paper over the cracks. If the property is damp, for instance, the problem will have to be sourced and eradicated, otherwise doing any kind of internal decoration will be a waste of time and money. A cosmetic refurbishment is generally done on a house that is basically in good repair, but is dated and in need of modernisation and a general overhaul.

Furniture

If you are aiming to sell your home, you will already have a furnished property. It will be important for you to consider whether the property is over furnished. If the house looks cluttered with furniture, this will give the impression that the house is not spacious. As space sells property you will want to avoid this. If necessary, you should consider putting some of your furniture in storage. This may seem a costly exercise but if it will help you to achieve the full market value for your property, this will make economic sense. Similarly, if your furniture is large, dated or past its sell by date and you are moving somewhere smaller you could try and sell it at auction, and, if necessary hire some furniture on a monthly basis, until you sell your property. If you don't want to do either of those things there are simple ways that you can improve the look of your property.

The carpet

If you don't want to go to the expense of putting in a new carpet and providing the carpet is not too stained or shabby looking, there is no need to, but you should at least make sure the carpets are cleaned. Smells may lurk (particularly if you have pets) that could put off potential buyers and stains will look unsightly. If the carpets are 'swirly' or heavily patterned, then you would be wise to consider replacing them, as these will affect the overall look of the property and make it look 'busy', which is something you want to avoid. Similarly, if the carpets are dark this will also have an affect on the overall look of the property, as most buyers are looking for a clean, fresh look.

The three piece suite syndrome

If your comfy sofa and favourite chair are beginning to look a little tired and you don't want to replace them at this stage, prior to your move, you can always jazz these up inexpensively, with throws and cushions.

Kitchens

Kitchens are an important part of any refurbishment plan, be it a cosmetic make over or a total re-design. A kitchen does not need all mod cons to make it look good. It helps, but if the budget can't run to it, there are other ways to spruce up a kitchen.

♦ Cupboard doors can be painted. If you paint the doors in an egg shell based paint they can easily be wiped down. Paint them in a pale colour so they do not dominate the kitchen.
♦ Change the handles on the units for something more contemporary.
♦ If the work surfaces are past their sell-by date they will have to be replaced. This can be done cheaply by using laminate.
♦ The cooker. Quite often all a tatty looking cooker needs is a good clean . . . so get your oven cleaner out!
♦ Paint the walls a light, fresh colour as this helps give the kitchen a clean image.
♦ If there is a window in the kitchen put in a blind. This will help give the kitchen a cleaner line.
♦ If the floor covering is marked and shoddy looking, replacing it with linoleum is an economical option. There is a vast range to chose from but, again, go for something neutral and understated. You do not want to inflict your taste upon a potential buyer.
♦ A few pictures can add a touch of colour and can also be removed easily.
♦ A brightly coloured tea towel, oven gloves, apron and accessories can add that designer touch.

Little things mean a lot

When presenting a property that you are trying to sell, think of adding small things that will enhance it, rather than large things which will overwhelm it. Fresh flowers, fruit in a fruit bowl, all add that touch of colour and help with that creative touch.

Bathrooms

There are no short cuts where bathrooms are concerned. They have to look presentable, but it is possible to make them look that way without having to replace everything.

- If the bath is chipped it may be possible to re-enamel it rather than have it replaced.
- If the sink looks uninspiring or old fashioned, maybe all it needs is a change of taps and a good clean!
- If the tiles are not cracked and are in reasonable condition you could always re-grout them to give them a fresher look.
- Display an attractive mirror.

If you have to renovate an old bathroom rather then put in a new one, accessorise it by adding a colour coordinated soap dish, toothbrush holder, bath mats and towels.

Decorating for selling

When selling a property, a fresh lick of paint can make all the difference but keep the decorative finishes neutral. Creams and whites are the best option, as they will allow the purchaser to see the property without someone else's decorative stamp on it. If you paint the walls in the colours of your choice, you may alienate a potential buyer. Neutrally decorated properties also make the rooms look bigger, as dark colours close a room in. What you are trying to sell is the space and, therefore, it is common sense to show the space in the most flattering light.

Gardens

Ignore gardens at your peril, particularly your front garden, as that is where your potential purchaser will form their first opinion of the property. It's called 'kerb appeal' and if the front of your house looks unkempt and overgrown, it will not help make a good first impression and could put buyers off. Similarly, with the back garden, make sure that the lawn is cut, hedges are trimmed and the borders are not overgrown with weeds. If the patio area looks dirty, clean it with a pressure pump. If it still looks dull, cheer it up with some pots of brightly coloured flowers . . . you can always take these with you when you move.

CHOOSING AN ESTATE AGENT

The next step on the roller coaster of selling your property will be to appoint an estate agent. Estate agents are a necessary part of the property market and there are a lot of them out there. It is important that you choose the right one when selling your property. Anyone can set themselves up as an estate agent, so even if they appear to have all the trappings; flashy offices, headed notepaper and a website, they may not have the track record to go with it. If you decide to sell your property privately you will need to decide on the price you want and take out the necessary advertising in the newspapers or on the Internet. If you appoint an estate agent it will be their job to value your property and I would recommend getting at least three valuations.

Valuations

Do not necessarily choose the agent that gives the highest valuation as it is important to remember that they want to lure you into an exclusive 'sole agency' agreement. They may well give you a high valuation in order to secure the contract and it is common for estate agents who give high valuations to lower the asking price after a couple of weeks. It is important you research the market yourself and get an idea of what is an appropriate price for your property.

- Get three valuations.
- Ask to see terms and conditions.
- Ask what advertising methods the agent employs.
- Check what their commission rate is.
- Choose a local estate agent (they will know the local market).

- After agreeing which agent you are choosing, enter a 'sole agency agreement' as this will save on commission.

Commission

The commission rate can vary from agency to agency and from area to area. It can range from 1% to 3%. If the commission rate is high, negotiate it down. I have always negotiated on the commission charges and although the reduction may only be 0.25%, it is worth having, as the commission charges can stack up quite high on an expensive property. Even if the property is not expensive, it's still worth negotiating on the commission. Make sure any reductions are put in writing, and if you are going 'sole agency', set a time limit on the 'sole agency' agreement (six weeks) and have this written into the contract. If you are not satisfied with the agent's efforts after the agreed contract time expires, you can try another agent and enter another 'sole agency' agreement without incurring multiple agency charges (which can be significantly higher).

Good estate agents

There are a choice of several organisations which a reputable estate agent should belong to and they are:

- National Association of Estate Agents (NAEA): 08701 4381810 or www.naea.co.uk.
- Association of Residential Letting Agents (ARLA): 01494 431 1680 or www.arla.co.uk.
- National Approved Letting Scheme (NALS): www.nalscheme.co.uk.
- Royal Institute of Chartered Surveyors (RICS): 0870 333 1600 or www.rics.org.

Membership of these organisations does not necessarily mean that they are 'perfect' estate agents, but it does mean that there are certain standards they must adhere to in order to be members of any of these professional bodies.

Property description

Once you have instructed an agent, they will draw up the property details. Ask to see a copy of this before the property is marketed and if you think you can add any useful suggestions to the description, or the property is not being accurately described then don't be afraid to put your ideas forward. Remember that an agent's description may not always be perfect but generally they will know how to describe a property better than you can and highlight what its selling points are. They will also know the limitations of their advertising space. Remember, it is an estate agent's job to sell your property and they are likely to describe your property in the most flattering terms. I remember a property being described as having a paved garden area, only to discover it had only a small slab of concrete outside the back door!

Advertising

It is an agent's job to advertise your property in newspapers, property journals and on their website. Marketing is the area that costs the agent most money and it does not necessarily result in a sale. It is also an estate agent's job to provide good property details, preferably including colour pictures. If you are undecided about an agent, ask to see examples of their property details. Do they look well presented? Check to see what papers they advertise in and examine how they present the properties and what size their advertising space is. If they have a website (and it is my view that they all should) then look it up on the Internet. Ask how often it is updated. Check out other agents' websites and compare them. This is a good way of comparing property prices too! A useful website to find estate agents in a chosen area is www.yell.com.

SUMMARY

It may seem like a lot of trouble to go to in order to sell a house, but what you are trying to guarantee is a speedy sale to the right buyer at the right price. Once you have made the decision to downsize and move to somewhere that you feel is more manageable, you will want to get on with it. The last thing you want is a dated, tired looking house, languishing on the market for months at an inflated price. There is a lot of competition for buyers and you will need to steal an edge on the market if you are to avoid constantly having to drop your asking price due to lack of interest. It makes sense to spend a little and save a lot, by aiming to get the full asking price.

Epilogue

I first began researching 'retirement living' when I was looking for a retirement home for my mother. I was amazed to discover all the opportunities there are for elderly people looking for a more stress free and active retirement, free from the burdens of home maintenance, security and health issues. It seems only fitting that my mother should have the last word on this, so I asked her to write a piece to include in the book and here it is.

It was whilst sitting on the seafront in Whitstable that I made the momentous decision to downsize. I was living in a Yorkshire village at the time, not far from where I was born. I had lived in the same house for 51 years, 23 of them on my own after my husband's death. Prior to that it was a family home, shared by husband, son, daughter and dog!

My only daughter had moved to London and my son lived in a different part of Yorkshire, so I was used to living alone and making all my own decisions. However, I was not getting any younger and was beginning to have health and mobility problems. As a result of this, it was getting increasingly difficult for me to manage my house, particularly as I was having difficulty going upstairs.

I was lucky enough to have a network of helpers, but the responsibility of maintaining the property was a considerable drain, both mentally and financially. Both my children were concerned about me living in such a large house, alone and in failing health.

I loved my home, having lived in it for so long. It was full of memories and I truly believed I would never leave it and that I would continue to manage somehow.

Whilst I was sitting on the seafront in Whitstable, looking out to sea, I thought there had to be an alternative. I knew that it was time to make the decision to leave my home, before I was forced into leaving it for health reasons.

My daughter and I started looking for a retirement home . . . a stress free environment closer to where she lived, so she could offer me back up and support when needed. We were lucky to find a delightful little retirement apartment very close by which was perfect, having all the benefits of sheltered accommodation, whilst offering independent living.

It was an enormous upheaval and very traumatic for me to leave my home. My furniture was too big and I had accumulated a lot of possessions over the years. So, most of it went to auction and house clearance sales, whilst a lot of other items went into black bin bags for the charity shop and the hospice.

The estate agent was very helpful and after several months on the market my home was finally sold. After that there was the preparation for the actual move and the organisation that went with it, such as informing utility companies, arranging the removal and dealing with the legal side, all of which was stressful.

However, it was soon over and I settled into my new home . . . what bliss! No more maintenance worries. Companionship when I needed it and peace and quiet when I didn't. Moving to London has been an enormous change for me, but I am very happy and settled in my retirement apartment.

My only regret is that I didn't do it sooner!

Sylvia Hulley

Annie Hulley's Web Page

For up to date information on:

Property . . . what's hot and what's not, where to live and what to buy?

Finance . . . can I afford it and what are my options?

Lifestyle choices . . . such as should I retire abroad or travel the globe?

These questions and many more can be answered by visiting www.anniehulley.com for news, views, advice and information.

Index

How To Books are available through all good bookshops, or you can order direct from us through Grantham Book Services.

Tel: +44 (0)1476 541080
Fax: +44 (0)1476 541061
Email: orders@gbs.tbs-ltd.co.uk

Or via our website

www.howtobooks.co.uk

To order via any of these methods please quote the title(s) of the book(s) and your credit card number together with its expiry date.

For further information about our books and catalogue, please contact:

How To Books
Spring Hill House
Spring Hill Road
Oxford OX5 1RX

Visit our web site at

www.howtobooks.co.uk

Or you can contact us by email at info@howtobooks.co.uk